BIBLE
RELATIVITY

BIBLE RELATIVITY

Rondo A. Murphy

To order additional copies of this book, contact:
Xlibris Corporation
1-888-7-XLIBRIS
www.Xlibris.com
Orders@Xlibris.com

CONTENTS

INTRODUCTION

Few people like to write about biblical prophesy because has been a sore spot to christian down through the ages. It seems to become source material for the cults. Besides, it really adds little to the salvation message, so most christian sects would like to ignore the subject.

Since 1948, when the Jews established a new nation, we entered a new era prophesied by God that knowledge would be increased (Dan. 12:4). If we apply our modern knowledge to biblical prophesy today, we find it follows a uniform plan.

Truth cannot refute truth, and to find truth, one must first understand what is real. For many centuries the Bible has been mysterious about Old Testiment prophesy. Even the Jews stumbled over it. Some mysteries are there due to the frailties of men. Other prophesies do not reveal themselves clearly until we approach our end time era. That is why the Book of Daniel was very confusing. It, along with other Bible prophesy, could not be understood until earth's history nears its end. We now enter that era when all things can be understood (Amos 3:7).

Down through the centuries the salvation message has been perpetuated by an emotional appeal. This has worked well because it appeals to people to get on a emotional high. They like to remain in their comfort zone in spite of the fact the Bible encourages them to progress with wisdom and knowledge (Rom.10:2). Knowing leads us to a relationship of trust with the Lord.

Without knowledge we can not explain to ourselves, nor to others, how the Deity works. We can not separate the eternal from our natural. Jesus said: "Why do ye not understand my speech? Because ye cannot hear my word. Ye are of your father the devil, and the lust of your father ye will do" (Jn. 8:43–44). That means one must separate fact from fiction. Even in the Bible. Bear in mind that Abraham did his own thing when he lay with Hagar. He lacked trust in the Lord. Abraham had to demonstrate his trust later with the life of his son Isaac. To progress no further than the emotional can become a stumbling block to us (Jer. 6:21; 1 Col. 8:9). Jesus explains it well: He that is able to receive it, let him receive it" (Mt. 19:12).

This book is very revealing in many aspects of the Bible. It will demonstrate original ideas from biblical scriptures. Some will receive it while others will not. Because it might threaten their comfortable zone.

PROLOGUE

"All scripture is given by inspiration of God, and is profitable for doctrine, for reproof, for correction, for instruction in righteousness" (II Tim. 3:16).

"Beloved, believe not every spirit, but try the spirits whether they are of God: because many false prophets are gone into the world" (1 Jn. 4:1).

"Give instructions to a wise man, and he will be yet wiser: teach a just man, and he will increase in learning. The fear of the Lord is the beginning of wisdom: and the knowledge of the holy is understanding" (Proverbs 9:9–10).

"My people are destroyed for lack of knowledge: because thou hast rejected knowledge, I will also reject thee, that thou shalt be no priest to me: seeing thou has forgotten the law of thy God, I will also forget thy children" (Hosea 4:6).

"Follow after charity, *and desire spiritual gifts*, but rather that ye may prophesy" (I Cor. 14:1). "But he that prophesieth speaketh unto men to edification, and exhortation, and comfort" (I Cor. 14:3). "…I shall speak to you either by revelation, or by knowledge, or by prophesying, or by doctrine" (I Cor. 14:6). How is it then brethren? when ye come together, every one of you hath a psalm, hath a doctrine, hath a revelation, hath a interpretation. Let all things be done unto edifying" (I Cor. 14:26).

THE CREATION

There is a gap in time between Genesis 1:1 and Genesis 1:2. The possibility has been known for centuries, but to suggest it to be factual, flares against general established Christian thinking. But when considered, it does tend to clear up a lot of mysteries that surround the creation.

The present-day "gap" theory was perhaps originated by Thomas Chalmers of Edinburg University. He proposed it in 1814 to make room for the catastrophes that appear so evident in the earth's fossil record. Almost a hundred years later the theory was given circulation by George H. Pember, who published **Earth's Earliest Ages** in 1909. A most scholarly defense of the gap theory came as recently as 1970 by Arthur C. Custance when he published **Without Form and Void**.

The creation is strategically important to understand as divine literature. It lays a firm foundation underneath the many creative affirmations contained in both the Old and New Testaments. The creative subject should be attached to the mental status of any spiritual Bible reader, because it focuses God's power, and His divine authority to the rest of His scriptures. If it will not focus, do not use it.

Paul relates the deity and the life of Jesus direct to God's creative acts (Col. 1:15-19). "For the invisible things of him from the creation of the world are clearly seen, being being understood by the things which are made (Rom. 1:20).

The Bible is not infallible. Errors do creep into it because of the frailties of men (Errors in translations, and there have been additions); but when read with spiritual eyes, it does indeed contain the truth of what God intended for man in both the Old and New Testaments. It needs to be reinterpreted so that it can be seen in todays light. Man's ability to reason today is much greater than at any other time in our human history.

The Bible is purposely full of stumbling blocks as they are allowed there by God (Jer. 6:21). There was a huge block that threw the whole Jewish nation out of synchronization. The Jews did it to themselves. This book identifies those happenings. Events so disruptive that God chose to become a man and start a new and personal relationship with man?

The first four books of the Bible were written by Moses (Num. 33:2). There is some question about who actually wrote Deuteronomy? This question will be explored in detail later in this book. We mention it now because the religious attitude the book represents the first time God"s words have been tamper with in the Bible. What Deuteronomy does is definately obscure any notion about a prior world, populated by a spiritual people who accessed the physical.

The original, or first beginning is found in Job chapter 38. The second beginning is described in Genesis (Gn.1:3). We must understand that Genesis is a renewal, or a recreation of this earth for beginning of Adam and Eve. If William J. Bryan had known this he could have correctly answered Clearance Darrow's question at the Scopes trial in 1923. Mr. Bryan should have known that the sun was already there! It did not shine until the darkness was rolled back on the third day of renewed second creation.

In Isaiah 14:12; Jer. 4:23; and Ez. 14:14 refer back to the original creation when comparing God's pending destruction on Israel in 587 B.C. Much confusion is cleared up about these scriptures listed above when they are understood in content. They describe the actual battle that took place on the earth in ancient times. How that battle is finely won by God when He died at the cross. The whole scenario will be made known as this book moves along. Knowing makes faith easier.

It should be obvious that this earth has been inhabited by humans before. The Bible reader can not reconcile Job to todays world. Its anciently inspired. Glance through the book and one might determine a foreign demeanor. It does not fit in our world of today. Most of it religious expressions are very confusing to both Jew and Gentile. In Job we have a perfect creation. One where all "the sons of God [angels] shouted for joy" (Job 38:7). From what Job writes in 1:7, we can definitely assume Satan was in charge. Very little is said about Job's human inhabits and life styles. The book of Job chief concern is about a rift between God and Satan. Though obscure, it reveals another human creation before Adam.

What places the book of Job outside of our present world is the way people are saved. This human race are saved according to their own righteousness (Job 6:9; 8:6; 29:14; 33:26; 36:3. In the world we live in now, we are saved by our faith in HIS righteousness (That is what the atonement is all about), and we are saved according to His grace (Eph. 2:5–8).

A new concepts, like intelligent humans lived on earth during prehistory; frees the mind for many wild imaginations. Perhaps it was they who built the Sphinx and Stonehedge.

In the world of Job the flesh was submitted unto judgment. In our world we have God's righteousness to take away the sins of the flesh. Mercy was not a factor in Job's world because salvation was earned. God's ability to extend mercy, and to be merciful was a virtue Satan could not understand. Satan and God were bickering over this in Job. Satan was sure that mercy would rob justice. This would make God invincible and open to be overthrown. That quarrel continues on in our world Satan can not understand how God can be a merciful, forgiving, and a JUST God also.

When the prophet refers to the men of Job's world in Ezekiel 14, he identifies them as men who are saved by their own "righteousness" (v. 18). This mode of self living does deny God the chance to show grace. Thus, the expression must pertain to an inferior world very different from ours. We must rely upon God's grace in this world (Rom. 9:15). The hard thing for us to do is prove ourselves worthy. Salvation is a GIFT from God to those He may choose. God allowed evil to happen. To develope a more perfect man.

In Ezekiel chapter 14, he uses the names Job, Noah, and Daniel. Names familiar to us, but the situation applies to conditions found in Job's world. Job uses an expression very foreign to us: "The Lord gave, and the LORD hath taken away" (Job 1:21). Job was not a sinner. Therefore, Job's Lord, who took away, had to be someone with an attitude like Satan!

Using the name Satan would mean the Book of Job was written after the fact. "Lucifer", a very brilliant angel, lost his high station when he attempted to overthrow God. Later, "Lucifer" was changed to "Satan." (Meaning Adversary)

Genesis 1:1 describes earth's original creation. It depicts an all-sovereign and a resourceful God. Genesis 1:2 is another creation that restores the earth from a condition that had (HYAH) [became] "*Without form and void.*" Genesis 1:3 begins an account of that reshaping. A reshaping that takes advantage of many items that were already here from the original creation. In fact the second creation was more a rolling back the darkness and rejuvenating process.

Scholars and theologians argue the question, *When was the beginning?* The theologian Ussher suggests a beginning about 4004 BC. The modern scientific community tells us earth began 4,500,000,000 years ago. Perhaps they were both right.

This earth was created to be inhabited (Isa. 45:18). After God inhabited the earth, he placed Lucifer in charge. Lucifer rebelled, and as a result of his rebellion, the earth became "without form and void." God took action to stop Satan's rebellion by throwing his dominion earth into darkness. Later, God Himself prepares a garden in the midst of satan's dominion. This time God delegated authority to no one. God would take care of Adam and Eve, and their posterity by Himself.

Darkness has multiple meanings in the Bible. It is very unique to creation, and also in end time events (Isa. 45:7). "Darkness" is a term the Bible uses in a positive way for the agency of men. It certainly gives men the chance to evaluate the true light from God, as opposed to the eternal darkness prepared for satan. The darkness and the light are both now both present on earth. Job's world was different because there was not a choice between evil and good.

In Genesis, *darkness* is viewed as "waste" and "Void." Words that also describe the condition of those souls who will remain with a lust for sin at the great judgment day. Into this pit of waste and void will be Satan; plus his rebelling angels who questioned God's mercy in Job's world. Towards the end they will be bound until God finishes His work on this earth. Then comes the judgment and the final fate of the wicked.

I form the light, and create darkness: I make peace, and create evil: I the Lord do all these things" (Isa. 45:7). God has to be referring to Satan's creation, who scummed to evil. "God himself that formed the earth and made it; he hath established it, he created it not in vain, he formed it to be inhabited". Inhabit it he did. Perhaps in several increments of time. Today we are earth's final inhabitants, before the material universe is burned up.

Genesis 1:1 does not hint there is any other power that stands against God. Rather, it distinguishes God as absolute and external from His creation. All angels were present, and they all shared the excitement of God's original creation. For some strange reason the Book of Job has remained very precious to the Israelite people. It must predate their TORAH because other than the mention of burned offerings, the book does not follow the sacrificial law. Still, it has survived the establishment of the TORAH, and comes down through the annals of history to modern times. It is a small miracle that Job survives in its antiquity. It goes back to when the Jews lived God's impractical law of spiritual well being. That message went dead when the Book of Deuteronomy was found. That finding caused a religious revival and the Jewish TORAH LAW was established about 612 BC.

The Book of Job is an object lesson in ones struggle with Satan. That is why Lucifer's fallen name is used in the text. It was written after the fact, which means, after satan fell from God's grace. Job remains in the Bible as a means of edification. One must think about its foreign contents in order to derive its message (1 Cor. 14:33).

The Jewish revival should be a dark page in jewish history. Their true faith was set adrift. They drifted so far they came to lose all knowledge that Satan existed. Outside of the Book of Job, there are just two verses remaining about Satan in the Old Testament. This effects transcribing their own writings: "But the spirit of the Lord departed from Saul, and an evil spirit from the Lord troubled him" (I Sam. 16:14). Lost knowledge left God to blame for everything.

The Book of Job is seldom used. It begins by depicting Satan in communication with God at the highest level. Such a lofty position illustrates the high influence Satan once had with God. It shows a Satan without any restrictions. One who has authority and dominion. Jesus confirms that Satan still has the earth as his dominion (Jn. 14:30; 16:11). If this be so, all men since Adam have become a pawn in one big heavenly feud. God's will show that His wisdom is greater than the cunning of the devil. God uses this feud to buffet us and develop us to think freely.

The Bible tells us Satan was once called "Lucifer" (Isa. 14:12). The name denotes a position of high divine rank (Ez. 28:15). If Lucifer retains authority over this earth after he attemped his take-over from God, he can not be judged yet? Just confined to earth awaiting judgement. Jesus broke his hold over man when He was crucified on the cross (1 Cor.2:7), but judging Satan awaits the day of judgments at the end of the world (Rev. 20:10–15).

Since Lucifer is still "prince" of this earth, we may safely assume the battle once fought in heaven has now been confined to the aurora of this earth (Rev. 12:9). God creates a paradise in Satan's dominion, and with Adam He penetrates a portion of earth. God asks Adam to subdue the rest of the earth, but Adam blew it and fell into Satan's grip. This time it would not be necessary to cause a deep freeze on earth, because God now had a contingency plan. A way to retrieve man from his fallen predicament (Gen. 3:15).

A time gap in God's plan makes the Bible scriptures agree with the catastrophes etched in our rock strata around the world. This earth has been shaped and then reshaped, often *violently*! Psalms 104:30 suggests that David was keenly aware this earth had only been *renewed* to fit its present condition. The Bible suggest if has been washed, and has undergone some atmospheric changes.

After exposing light, God "divided" the waters above and below the earth (Gen. 1:7). The early atmosphere must have been conducive for long human life the way those old timers lived to be almost a thousand years old.

Read what Genesis says about the land mass (Gen. 1:9). It suggests a single land mass around the equator. Before the flood our earth might have been a tropical paradise. After food of Noah the Bible indicates a climatic change. For the first time the earth experiences a rainbow (Gen. 9:13).

Scientific plate technology upholds the biblical idea that the land mass was all one piece prior to the flood. The flood is a catastrophic event. Some scientists are starting to realize that there are great surges of growth in earth's past. Catastrophic events did occur in earth's past, and the earth has not always had a slow, steady, and predictable kind of an evolution.

In both creations, God at first did it perfectly. God has been obligated to make some changes owing to the way men tend to succumb to evil. In the beginning God created perfectly. If this were not so, God would be infallible and not capable to remain God (Ps. 18:30; 2 Sam. 22:31; Mt. 5:48). When God is through with the agency of man, He will again render the earth perfect for His thousand year reign (Ez. 38:20).

God uses Satan to develop man in a more positive and productive way. Satan's opposition fits nicely to enhance the human development towards a condition of genuine love and appreciation. We now have a world arena where man can be made thought worthy by their own human instincts. Being made thus thought perfect, we all can learn to rely upon God for eternal love beyond knowledge available to us. To know Him is to trust Him. Faith without trust is meaningless (James 2:24). Satan destroys your faith by attacking your trust. Satan likes to take away your health and belongings.

Yes, the earth always *was* since its original creation. In fact it is still here, and shows the evidence of many violent upheavals down through the ages. There have been many delays along the way, but God says: "Remember the former things of old (Isa. 46:9). "Declaring the end from the beginning, and from ancient times the things that are not yet done, saying, My counsel shall stand, and I will do all my pleasure (Isa. 46:10).

Something definitely happened to this earth to make it become without form and void. God certainly did not create it that way. Open rebellion by Lucifer caused it to [become] "without form and void." That ancient rebellion continues as Adam and Eve were persuaded to rebel against God.

When Satan destroyed the perfect man (Jesus) he placed himself under God's direct judgment (See 1 Cor. 2:8). With the resurrection Satan's power over death were broken. Now Satan is restricted by the spiritual power Jesus is able to place within man. That spirit fell upon the earth at Pentecost (1 Cor. 2:8). This comforting spirit will remain until it is Raptured off the earth at the return of Jesus.

Satan's full power will be restored to him when the Holy Ghost is called back into heaven (2 Thes. 2:7). Those who attach themselves to the Holy Ghost will become transfigured and caught to meet Jesus when he spirit leaves. At that time Satan will again be able to perform miracles and great tricks. Even to the extent that some will be fooled into accepting him as God.

In the Book of Job, we find a people who were directly responsible to both God, and their earth-ruling lord (Satan). Their mode of salvation, of course, had to be different from ours. They had earth's material animals to give them fear and wisdom. Simply maintaining goodness gave these men and women their under-standing (Job 28:28). Unlike Job, we should not fear today what man or beasts may do to us (Ps. 56:4, 118:56) but only our own association with evil thoughts and deeds.

The Book of Job explains the details about earth's original creation (Job ch. 38, 39, 40, 41). Job tells us that when the earth was first made, all the angelic hosts of heaven were present. Those angels "sang together" at the thought of earth being created. We do not find this same scenario in Genesis. The only singing to be found during the earth's renewal for the creation of Adam was perhaps a sour note from Satan as he persuaded Eve to disobey God.

Former things for us to remember is that the heavens shook and the earth trembled (Job 9:6). Unlike the Jews, we should remember "former things" as they pertain to the fall of Satan from his high ranking position over earth. It is strange, but more and more, we are finding Christians who no longer believe in Satan.

Compare the down trodden Job to Adam's commandment to "subdue and have dominion" over the earth. Look at the authority given to Israel's high priests in Ex. 28:30; & Lv. 8:8. Intense reading of Job reveals that Satan questions God's motives concerning man as man's presence is of little consequence. What is valuable to understand in Job is that these two omnipotent beings became embroiled in a dispute that wound up in a challenged to God's own holiness. Thus God isolated Satan to this earth (Rev. 12:9), and here the battle continues. Satan needs to be judged, shown that he is indeed in error, before God can justly his total banishment. Satan has to be shown that his way of rule is a degradation. Satan rules by force while God's ways are through

Before God judges Satan, He will use him to temper Adam and the descendants of Adam. Being be born into this world of sin does tend to set one apart from the blessings of God. God is no respecter of persons (Acts 10:34). A strong belief based upon knowledge and obedience is most acceptable to God.

Each person born is predestined to return unto God (Eph 1:5–11). God rolled back the darkness that covered the earth with full knowledge of man's predestiny after Adam and Eve were created. He allows some things from Job's world to remain—like the devil in charge, along with other items that we will go into later, but when Moses wrote Genesis, he explains that Adam would be in the image of God (Gen. 1:27).

The scriptures are very clear about the way Satan once sought to overthrow the throne of God (See Isa. 14:12–23). Failure to understand the Book of Job weakens our whole understand about the workings of God. Many Christians can not make out Revelations 12:9. The revelation describes the plight of Israel with a flash back to Satan's fall long ago. Angels were cast out with him. Where were they cast to? *To the earth* where they make trouble for Israel (Rev. 12:4).

"Knowledge" is used by Peter seven times in the first eleven verses of 2nd Peter. The Greek word it derives from is **"epignosts"**, which means "full knowledge of a mature kind". Read these first eleven verses carefully and one can see where Peter reveals a prior world. "Whereby the world that then was, being overflowed with water, perished" (11 Peter 3:6). No this is not the time of the flood because the world did not parish. It continued after the flood waters receded. What Peter saw was the earth just before it was frozen, darkened, and made void. The next verse (7), Peter talks about things "which are now".

In his writings Peter admits to stirring up "your pure minds by way of remembrance" (11 Peter 3:1). About things spoken before the prophets. This makes the Book of Job truly unique. What it has to say pre-dates even Genesis according to Peter. It stays in the Bible for those who have "pure minds", or enough wisdom about Godliness, to understand what the rift was about between God and Satan.

Satan thought God to be too merciful. Satan showed no mercy and thought everyone should be treated the same. God showed favoritism and to Satan this was imperfection. In Satan's mind, God was imperfect, and therefore should no longer be God. We, of this world, are given choice. The Bible will help us if we will just fine what mercy is about.

Satan was here when God created Adam. He was here to tell man he would *not* die if he ate the forbidden fruit. Yes, man could become knowledgeable by learning good from evil. The real deception was the lie that man would not die! Man did die a spiritual death, leaving the physical body of clay with only the soul. A very weakened defense mechanism in Satan's dominion. Until Jesus made God's spirit available to dwell with man again (Eph. 2:14).

By birth, man is created lower than the angels (Heb. 2:7), but to those who overcome death, they will be appointed to rule over the angels (See 1 Cor. 6:3). This illustrious potential is what really infuriates Satan to his hateful jealousy. In all his prior majesty, he was not created with this mortal potential. Man, by being created in the image of God, is potentially superior to Satan and the fallen angels of heaven (I Cor. 6:3). Each individual who has lived since Adam had the potential to gain a higher place in God's sight than the angels created before the earth was originally formed.

In the Book of Job Satan is depicted as having authority over men. His authority over men has greatly diminished when he is found tempting Eve in the garden of Eden. He no longer had welcome access to the high council of heaven. In the Garden of Eden, Satan needed the aid of an animal to approach men. He held no authority over man until they were persuaded to sin. As sin entered, paradise was taken away, leaving them to travail in pain and sorrow as they were transfigured to dwell in a physical body.

After the fall of man, God committed to Eve, that He would not abandon man (See Gen. 13:15). This should reassure men there is yet a destiny which would take man back into the presence of God. Satan will manage to delay things, but as God says: "So shall my word be that goeth forth out of my mouth: it shall not return unto me void, but shall accomplish that which I please, and it shall prosper in the thing whereto I sent it" (Isa. 55:11).

Satan was correct when he said man would come into the knowledge of "Good and Evil." Endowed by God with His living soul (Ez. 18:4), that gives us the ability to seek out His loving Spirit, which in turn makes us whole (I Thes. 5:23).

Long before the heavens, and the earth were created, God had a specific plan and purpose for this earth. The fossil record indicates that the earth has been used for inhabitation many times. We also know from the fossil record that God retained many animal species from the earliest of times. Some were in Job's world and ours too.

God's highest creation and greatest expectancy rests with the creation of a free moral agent that makes us different from all other animals. Created with the ability to determine our own destiny, and imparted with God's eternal soul (Gen. 2:27). A life giving essence that has an infinity for the eternal living God (Ez. 18:4). And one which will remaind eternally mixed up if it does not find its maker.

Do not be afraid of prophecy. In fact, God asks us to "desire" and to "covet" prophecy (1 Cor. 14:1–39). "...I am thy fellow-servant, and of thy brethren that have the testimony of Jesus: worship God: *For the testimony of Jesus is the spirit of prophecy*" (Rev. 19:10). God does not speak in secret (Isa. 45:19, 48:16; Amos 3:7), and all is laid out in his word, available for those who take the time to understand it.

As we approach the last days, the prophet Joel says God promises to "...pour out my spirit upon all flesh; and your daughters shall prophesy, your old men shall dream dreams, and your young men shall see visions" (Joel 2:28). One cannot remain ignorant of God's plan for men and expect to become privileged to spiritual insight about events to happen the last days (Study Rom. 10:2–3).

For hundreds of years after Jesus died, Christian people gathered in secrecy. They freely association with one another and learned about Jesus. The evidence suggests that each was capable to approach God individually. They met with each other and exchanged God's spiritual gifts they had received.

By 325 BC a segment of the church in Rome was accepted and legalized at the Council of Nicene. From out of this council there developed a parliamentry system of control. As the church gained this power they became final authority on what was true. Independent thinking became discouraged.

Free thinking became heresy after Christianity became a state religion under the Roman Emperor Constantine. The church as a body, limited individuality as authority became delegated to the top. The masses no longer had the ability to "prove all things" (I Thes. 5:21). The church claimed the succession to the key doctrines (Mt. 16:18–19) and the early epistles (Acts 15:23), and in doing so, became superior in directing God's kingdom (Spirit) on earth.

Thus Christianity encumbered itself with a huge amount of thought control. They also became all authority on what is true. If the church said the horse had 38 teeth in their mouth, and a person looked into the horses mouth and found they only had 36, the horse was wrong and the church was right.

Nothing new came out of the Bible when the Americas were discovered. The churches conservative authority would not review the covenants God made to a remnant of Israel: "Moreover I will appoint a place for my people Israel, and I will plant them, that they may dwell in a place of their own, and move no more" (See Sam. 7:10). America has been that place God is talking about in this scripture. We will will develop this more in another chapter.

The door of communication is open to all individuals who will put trust in their thoughts and prayers. Just remember "truth cannot refute truth". Direct prophesy ended with John's revelations, but under God's direction, anyone is capable if interpellating the scriptures. Seek to know the promises God made to Abraham, Isaac, Jacob. What Jacob promised his twelve sons. Then try to remember that all things written by God's spirit must be fulfilled (Lu 21:22).

What about all the promises to the "Gentiles" in the Bible (Lu. 21:24)? Who are the Gentiles Luke is talking about? Few realize that they are the Christ's "other sheep" (Jn.10:16), and they are chiefly located in that planted place Samuel talks about.

Are we now entering an era when men will "turn away their ears from the truth, and shall be turned unto fables" (2 Tim. 4:4). If you feel anger toward new ideas you could be there already. "As for my people, children are their oppressors, and women rule over them" (Isa. 3:12).

The Gentile age Luke refers to in (Lu 21:24) will end with a great world conflict Ezekiel talks about in Ez. Ch. 38 and 39. There are other prophesies to be fulfilled to bring this War on. One of these events is that the Gospel "must be published among all nations (Mr. 13:10). We shall also see the demise of capitalism (Ez. 7:19). Such chaos in the world will cause the Jews throughout the world to scurry back to their Jewish homeland in Palestine. Can we realize how all these troubles will eventually cause the world to resort back to the political status it was under during ancient Rome. These topics will be discussed in detail in the ensuing chapters of this book.

We will enlarge upon Daniel's prophecies as they become the framework for all other prophesy. How all the prophesy concerning the lost ten tribes and the Jews to receive salvation is still contained in the book (Bible). Isaiah saw the day when all sould read the book: "Seek ye out of the book of the Lord, and read: no one of these shall fail, none shall want her mate: for my mouth it hath commanded, and his spirit it hath gathered them" (Isa. 34:16). Dose it not seem strange that God directs us to read His book in the last days. God COMMANDS it! This commandment has to be for last days, because books have not been available to everyone until recently. Mark fulfills prophesy when he declares the book to be "published among all nations." Isaiah declares those who seek it out with the promise that "no one of these shall fail." When we think of it, God seeks to return spiritual thinking to it rightful place by leaving instructions to handle it approximately 700 years BC. Books will not become readily available until this the last days. We should free ourselves from mans learning for they are "ever learning, and never able to come to the knowledge of the truth" (II Tim.3:7).

"THOU RENEWEST
THE EARTH"

"But beware of Men: for they will deliver you up to the councils, and they shall scourge you in their synagogues" (Mt. 10:17). Most people read scripture like this and feel only emotion. They do not grasp its message. For one thing, God does not like the synagogue system. They indoctrinate rather than educate. **They tend to stifle a persons ability to think outside the norm. Some Christian Churches now fall in to this category.** One is just not allowed to think above the level of the group. Jesus was thrown out of His own synagogue when He offered something new (Lu. 4:18–29). They sought to kill Jesus. "And **ye shall be hated of all men for my name's sake:** but he that endureth to the end shall be saved (Mt. 10:22). Common sense is the ability to grasp that which is real, and hold on to it until the end. God would like you more if you were either "hot" or "cold", but He does not like it when you just go along with the group (Rev. 3:15–19).

God is explicit in Genesis 1:25 when He says He created "everything." This would have to include the dinosaurs too. Therefore, to read Genesis 1:25 correctly, one must conclude there is a prior creation, or accept the scientific theory of evolution. There is no doubt that the dinosaurs existed. Some creatures like the alligator and the whale are still alive on earth today. How did they survive 65 million years without evolving in some way, or were they resuscitated when When God renewist the earth for the second time?

We have the technology today to understand some of the past. But we remain ignorant of God's words when the Bible clearly depicts times when God is willing to erase time and start over again. It seems no one since Jerome in 400 AD has bothered to observe how the Bible presents a clearer picture as to world moves closer to its God intended goals. Those few who did during the dark ages were killed. Some who do today remain silent, and justly so. Jesus tells us not to cast our pearls before swine (Mt. 7:6).

The clearest evidence to support the time-gap theory is found in the writings of Jeremiah (Jer. 4:23–27). "I beheld the earth, and, lo, it was without form, and void; and the heavens, and they had no light" (V. 23). Verse 24 tells us the mountains trembled, and verse 25 says "man," and the "birds" had "fled" the earth. Verse 26 says: "the cities thereof were broken down." This vision shows the earth before God rolled back the darkness. In its "void" stage.

"For thus hath the Lord said, The whole land shall be desolate; yet will I not make a full end" (V. 27). God was displeased with the Jews when He gave this vision to Jeremiah? God compares his "destruction" of the whole earth to what He intended upon the Jewish nation. God was to alter course with His chosen people (Jer. 1:10).

The priests at that time were in the process of altering God's word He gave them though Moses. In 612 BC they wanted control over the prophets and kings. Indeed, Moses wrote the first four books of the Bible (Num. 33:2), but now the priests claimed new writings from Moses were found in the temple. They Canonized the new book against dire warnings by Hildah the prophetess: "Thus saith the Lord, Behold, I will bring evil upon this place, and upon the inhabitants thereof even all the curses that are written in the book which they have read before the king of Judah" (II Cron. 34:24). Evil soon did come upon the Jewish nation by the Babylonians just a few years after they established their "TORAH" Law. From 600 BC onward, the Jewish people have been in captivity one way or the other until 1948 AD.

A new nation status is prophesied for the Jewish people in the Bible. It is a sign post to mark the last generation before the tribulation period. The Jews have not yet set up orthodox worship, and will not til Jesus rebuilds the temple.

God was telling Jeremiah how he was going to destroy the ancient Jewish nation *without bringing them to a "full end"* (Jer. 4:27). There end will come in glory. Jeremiah was a prophet with a special commission: "See I have this day set thee over the nations and over kingdoms, to root out, and to pull down, and to destroy, and to throw down, to build, and to plant (Jer. 1:10). All of Jeremiah's writings indicate a severe spiritual drought for his people. God also uses Jeremiah to begin preparations for the New Covenant that would culminate with the birth and life of Jesus.

The Jewish people did lose their pride in 587 BC. They were defeated by the Babylonians. Fifty years after that, the Babylon were defeated by the Persians. King Syrus of Persia released the Jews to go back to Jerusalem. The sad part of it was, they reinstated their new TORAH Laws.

Daniel is their prophet during their Babylonian captivity. He assure them God is not through with them yet (Jer. 9:21). The angel Gabriel gave Daniel a promise from the Lord that re-affirms

Dan. 9:24–27, that He will not make a full end. In fact God determind a time when they would come into their glory (490 years). This count down began when the Jews returned to Jerusalem in 535 BC (Dan. 9:25).

Its true, 490 years has long sense come and gone, and once again God has altered time. This delay in time for the Jews came when Jesus came into the world. Jesus stopped the count down for the Jews and replaced the Old Testament law of sacrifice by grace (Matt. 9:17). Thus the 70 year weeks for the Jews was stopped at the end of the 69th week. Under grace, God completes the prophesy given to Jeremiah: "I will put my law in their inward parts, and write it in their hearts" (Jer. 31:33). So long as we have grace these words are still in effect. Under grace, God stands by all that is said right about the name of Jesus (Phil. 1:18).

How does all this apply to creation. It is a sample of how God works. Since there is opposition, and man became a free moral agent, there are times when the will of God is delayed. God's words do not return unto Him void because He stops to fix things. Jeremiah was called upon to rearrange the plight of Israel, and Daniel gave them a time table that also was delayed. At the end God's vows will become true to his chosen people. Right now they have been delayed: "For the vision is yet for an appointed time, but at the end it shall speak, and not lie: though it tarry, wait for it; because it will surely come, it will not tarry" (Hab. 2:3).

Adam's fall, the flood, and Israel's sojourn in the Sinai desert, are examples of the many setbacks man and God have undergone. Due to many human frailties it should not be hard to accept the fact the God has had men on this earth before.

We know from the flood of Noah that God uses all means to make it right in the end. At one time God entertained the idea to destroy Israel when they defies God's efforts to save them for the Egyptians. This when they opted to worship a calf (Ex. 32:10). Moses pleaded with God for the sake of the people, and God did relent on His intention to destroy them at that time (Ex.32:12). In the end God will fulfill His intention, but one may observe from scripture that God puts up with a lot from waffling from man. God extends many delays, but He has assured us that he always has the end in sight. One of God's greatest attributes is His patience.

Two items Jeremiah especially noted to be missing in his vision of a darkened earth are "men" and "winged fowl." Those items are back on earth in Genesis, and God is careful to make special mention of them (Gen. 1:21, 26).

Another item with special mention in these verses is the "whales." Why would God single out and mention whales? Perhaps God was dropping a clue that could be enlarged upon at a later date. A time when men had a capacity for greater knowledge of themselves and their special place in the world. Just recently we have discovered whale bones and are able to date them back to prehistory. By using the term "whale," God allows Genesis to agree with the truth made evident by todays scientists. They also say man is recent to this earth, while the whale has been here for millions of years. Thus the Bible allows the scientists to be correct in some of their data.

Genesis does not try to convey the impression that everything on this earth was created at once. In fact the opposite is true. The Bible story makes it clear that God created in several different phases. The mention of whales should, with today's knowledge, suggest that one phase of God's creation happened many eons ago. Jeremiah did not say this earth was barren when he saw it in its darkened state. The mention of "cities" suggests it was once full of activity.

When the earth was created initially there was a happy time in heaven (Job 38:7). "All the sons of God" (the angels) "shouted for joy" These words also describe a time in earth's prehistory before there was any rebellion in heaven. "All" angels did not shout for joy when God "renewest" this earth for the creation of Adam. The paradise garden of Adam and Eve was only a part of the earth. Satan controlled the rest.

Until the outpouring of knowledge in our day (Dan. 12:4; I Cor. 12:8), which comes upon men through the aid of the Holy Ghost (John 14:17–21), we are now able to assimilate more accurately the whole truth as it is revealed in the Bible. The reprobate mind can determine from rock strata that earth has undergone some very violent upheavals.

"For the invisible things of him from the creation of the world are clearly seen, being understood by the things that are made, even his eternal power and Godhead; so that they are without excuse" (Rom. 1:20). All the material evidence is here. By this handy work alone one can reason that there has to be a God. All we need to do is know Him.

Notice how Genesis puts the second creation into phases. There are separate days for the creation of animals, birds, whales, the subspecies, and then the herbs and grasses. What should become obvious is that "days" denote a separate increment of time. Some of these increments of time include animals created for the world of Job.

When God "renewest" the earth (Ps. 104:30), He retained some items from the first creation. Grass grew on the earth long before the sun appeared. We all know that photosynthesis can not take place without the ray of the sun. On the other hand, Job makes mention of some animals at his time that are no longer found on earth (Job 40:15–24).

Genesis does leave a lot to our imagination. The high mountains thrown up shows evidence of tropical vegetation. Even on the Antarctic continent. This evidence attest to a unified and temporal earth in the past. Science explains all this by admitting to one singe land mass in the past, but they deny a superior entity who could shove these land masses around the earth in the space of a much shorter time than millions of years.

Study in Genesis how herbs and grasses came from "yielding seeds" (Gen. 1:12). This answers the question of what came first— the chicken or the egg? In the Genesis creation, seeds had were already been planted on the earth, ready to yield! God does not say in Genesis that He creates seeds. God just asks them to yield. In the original creation described in Job, God created from nothing. But careful reading of Genesis indicates the earth has been used before.

David seems to be aware of a recreation when he writes Psalms 104:30. Did the chosen people, called Israel, lose this spiritual information some where in the past. The answer is "No." They just lost the meaning behind Job. But one might ask: How could they have this spiritual knowledge in the first place. The answer lies with the early Aaronic priests. They were given a sacred breastplate known in the Bible as the Urim and Thummum (Ex. 28:30; Lv. 8:8). When these instruments were properly used, the priest had direct communication with God. Through errors that led to sin the Book of Job may have lost its spiritual message to the old Jewish priests, but the sacredness of the book has remained to hold this book as holy by the Jews down through the ages.

Ask yourself, did God actually part the Red Sea? Did he feed the children of Israel with Manna from heaven? Did Moses really tap a rock and bring forth water in the desert? Did someone called "Jesus" really call people from the dead? Did He stretch forth his hand and calm the storm? If God can do these minor miracles, why is it so hard to accept the notion that God rearrange this earth? The question is, did God renew this earth as the Bible supports, or did it indeed initially begin in 4004 B.C., as most theologians accept?

Let us follow the criteria Peter lays down for reading the Bible. "No prophecy is of any private interpretation" (II Peter 1:20). This means the Bible interprets itself! All truth must relate in some way to the Bible. For example, we cannot have the Bible saying in one place that we may save ourselves and then have the Bible countermand that it is Jesus who saves. Both examples must fit the Bible before we can accept any of the Bible to be inspired. For the Bible to work, we must first realize one phase pertains to the ancient world of Job, and the other pertains to a second creation described in Genesis. Otherwise the Bible describes a different method of salvation from one world as versus the other. Now, try to bare in mind, that it is not God, who is the author of confusion (1 Cor. 14:33). Therefore, there must be a creation, and a recreation, for the Bible to be factual.

Job's world would vary slightly from ours. The major difference was the way be which they could save themselves (See Job 6:9; 8:6; 29:14; 33:26; 36:3). To be in Job's world was more like being a servant (Job 7:1&2). Job's men learned by being oppressed (Job. 10:3;12:9). With Satan in charge, their Lord gives and takes away (Job 1:21). Yes, God may do this if He should choose, but in the world we live in, each of us have the ability to make choices. We are the author of our destinies. Every living soul is equipped to guide our own destiny. We decide what are merits shall be in the afterlife.

The Bible makes it obvious the Lord in authority over Job was Satan. It was Satan's idea to give and to take away. He pressed his point until he sought to overthrow God. Thanks to some sensible angels like Michael, Satan was repelled in his vicious endeavors (Rev. 12:7). Yes indeed, Michael shall prevail in the end of times as well (Dan.

12:1). One can assume Job's world to be very similar to the paradise that existed in the garden of Eden. Should Adam and Eve have remained in their state of paradise, they could have subdued Satan by pushing him off the earth (See Gen. 1:28). The difference being that Adam and Eve sinned, where Job did not. In Job's case, there was no provision for sin. It was God who allowed adversity to come upon Job.

When Adam and Eve partook of the Tree of Knowledge, they at first digressed from a state of paradise, because it was they who originated their sin. We must recognize this contrast. Because of their sins the Tree of Life was put off limits to them (Gen. 3:24), making them subject to their own sins, which in turn cut them off from the Spirit of God.

The Book of Job actually gives us a peek into the work of God. Since there was no sin, there was no need for a Savior. Nothing is presented on this. Only the words "burnt" offerings has anything to do with the Old Testament. The people of Job had a different set of religious values. Job seems to be compelled by circumstances.

One the other hand, Adam and Eve were placed into a world which was free. True, they brought restriction upon themselves through sin, but whose world did they drop themselves into? Satan's world of compulsion, just as he ran it for Job. A condition where we are oppressed and are told by the imps of hell that we must save ourselves. How do these imps approach us. Through the mouths of other men. In the way that God speaks through men under grace (Mk.13:11). We in our world today have a chance to achieve freedom for our souls once again. It is truth that sets us free, along with God's selective judgements (Rev. 20:7–15).

The fall of Adam put man back under the compulsive rule of Satan. God selected a chosen people He called "Israel" to be under His abiding care. They were to be an example to all the rest of the world. They rejected God to live under a king. God caved in to their desires and anointed king Saul. It was not long before they developed into a world empire under king David. Soon there after they began to backslide.

There are a few verses in Isaiah which bear out the fall of Satan from heaven. With the fall, the world is described as a "wilderness" (Isa. 14:17). Isaiah agrees with Jeremiah when he saw the same vision. Since Isaiah comes before Jeremiah, we find God's same frame of reference as He describes the same doom on the northern ten tribes of Israel headquarters at Samaria. Destruction did fall upon northern Israel in 721 B.C., some hundreds of years earlier. This is twice God gave the same vision (Isa. 14:12–17; Jer. 4:23–27).

After God allowed complete destruction to fall on northern, only the tribes of Benjamin and Judah were left. It was assumed that it would be they who would receive all the promises God made to Abraham, Isaac, and Jacob. Therefore, little attention was paid to Jeremiah's warnings in 587 B.C. While it was Jeremiah's duty to "root out, and to pull down, and to destroy" (Jer. 1:10), it was Isaiah's commission to assure Israel a glorious future would break (Isa. ch. 43).

The future Isaiah speaks about is all wrapped up in understanding God's "marvelous work and wonder" (Isa.29:14). This great event is already set in place since the time of Jesus. Through Jesus, God keeps His promises anciently made to the "offspring" of lost Israel, as Isaiah describes in Chapters 43, 44, and the first six verses of chapter 45. Ezekiel 37 helps to explain how both segments of Israel will come together again.

Meanwhile, God's marvelous work has been to spread a spiritual gospel. Since Jesus brought the Spirit into the world, all men can approach God on an individual basis. The result has been conversions, fulfilling God's promise to Abraham that his seed would become as numerous as the sands upon the seashore (Gen. 22:17). The intermingling of the lost tribes of Israel has melted into the whole western world.

Ezekiel was shown Job's former world and was tricky the way he describes it. He qualifies the prophecy by naming three men who are *saved by their own righteousness*? It is unusual the way these three men were given names so very familiar to men in this world. Besides Job, Ezekiel mentions the names "Noah" and "Daniel"

(Ez. 14:14). Notice how Ezekiel qualifies the location of where these three men are when he says: "...but deliver their own souls by their righteousness" (Ez. 14:20).

Six times in Ezekiel 14, he emphasizes an expression that should enable a thinking person to unlock who these men really are and where they have to reside. He explains that these three men lived *"In it."* In what? They lived in a world before Satan fell! In a world they shared with tremendously huge and "noisome beasts" (See Ez. 14:15)! They passed through the land, "and they spoil it!"

What these beasts were like is explained in Job 40:15. They were so large, they could drink up a "whole river." The only animals to fit this description are extinct. This verse in Job describes dinosaurs. Today, the western world has been given the ability to think freely, so new evidence is being presented. Whole fossilized skeletons were not analyzed until 1857. Instead of christendom themselves been looking for these items, they chose to deny them, leaving the scientific community to start a religion of their own. They give these discoveries a meaning. They call it "evolution."

Certain aspects about evolution fit the Bible. Bear in mind that the earth was made to be inhabited. It once was cleared of humans by a flood, the Bible tells us that (Gen. 7:17–24). Before that time Ezekiel tell us the earth was at another time stripped of all its human occupants (Ez. 14:16). It follows that God could have used this earth at one time for just dragons. But as God made this earth his "footstool" (Isa. 66:1), it also follows its present high position, and great agency of our present day men position.

Ezekiel's complete annilation of man has never happened in this world since Adam and Eve. Our reproductive process can be traced directly to Adam and Eve (Lu. 3:23–38). In fact, DNA science can trace our present human origin back to one single woman. If Isaiah, Jeremiah, and Ezekiel are correct, we must look for another prior human race, to support the strong biblical contention that one entire human race was annihilated. Read Jeremiah 4:24, Isaiah 14:17, and Ezekiel 14:16–18.

King David of ancient Israel seems to understand these unusual earthly factors. His writings in Psalms indicate he was very close to God. He describes this earth as being *renewed* (Ps. 104:30)! One does not renew something unless it existed before.

About this time you might ask why God did not make His use of this earth more clear? If He had, it would have confused earlier readers who felt the earth was the center of the universe. If we had a general consensus from all the people rather than interpretation from one or two men, God's work may have been faster. The general population still likes to rely on man, rather than his own spiritual faculties for truth. Going against the status quo makes the truth seeker ostracized in the world (Mt 1:13; Lu. 21:17).

Jesus acknowledges that pursuit of truth is not a very easy task: "Enter ye in at the strait gate: for wide is the gate, and broad is the way, that leadeth to destruction, and many there be which go in thereat: Because strait is the gate and narrow is the way, which leadeth unto life, and few there be that find it" (Mt. 7:13–14). Just hearing about Jesus can be fulfilling to the soul, but to refine it with understand sets one apart from the rest of the world. Always bear in mind, God must be worshipped in spirit (Jn. 4:24).

As scientists learn more about our material universe, they can see order in it. The experts now admit they think the whole universe had to be created in order to effect life as we know it on earth today. Some say it took exploding novas to mesh with our solar system and impregnate it with the necessary iron and chemicals to sustain our own animal bodies. You hear some say that we are made of star stuff. Without their knowing it, scientists agree with the way God organized the universe, everything to effect life upon this earth.

Some who read this may scoff as they point out that Job mentions Adam (Job 31:34). In Hebrew *Adam* simply means "the first man." The Adam described in Job hides "iniquity in his bosom." All our first Adam did was try to hide his nakedness. He did not understand iniquity at first.

Consider how casually Paul calls Jesus a living "Adam" (I Cor. 15:45). Jesus is the first man to raise from the dead. In this same scripture, Paul says there is a first, and a last Adam. This would be "Alpha" and "Omega" Jesus. All Job indicates to us was a first, or an Adam, to begin Job's world.

Satan is also a name that means "first," but it means first among the devils. Since the Book of Job was written after the fact, it can call Lucifer "Satan" (Job 1:9). Under the name "Lucifer" or before his fall, Satan did have access to the high councils of heaven. Under his fallen name "Satan," Lucifer no longer has this heavenly access, not when he has been confined to this earth (Rev. 12:9). If one does not put Job in context the authority of Satan becomes confusing to the casual Bible reader.

Satan is no longer at liberty to leave this earth. If he were not limited by God, and can roam to heaven as Job says, it seems to throw doubt upon God's ability to confine Satan during the millennium. God totally confines Satan at the millennium by merely turning the whole earth into a paradise (See Isa. 11:6–9; Jn. 16:3). Sure, faith and God's Spirit will be in this paradise, and it is also full of the "knowledge" of the Lord (Isa. 11:6:9).

So what are we looking for in this world? As much spiritual knowledge of the Lord as we can get. That is all we can take with us when we leave. Knowledge, and are own individual composure.

Sometimes the Bible sound as though the devil thwart God at various times in the Old Testament, but a more clear-eyed view of the scriptures will show us how everything the devil does is only permitted by God. Most of the time mans trouble is self deserving, because of the terrible sin he allows his blinded self to sink into (See Jer. 32:35).

We are able to look out into space today with a far greater grasp of its full magnitude. We can be sure God has used it in many other places. In fact Jesus admits that "In my Father's house are many mansions: if it were not so, I would have told you. I go prepare a place for you (Jn. 14:2). One can only speculate about how much of the universe is under God's usage. This we do know. That we humans are made in the express image of God, and therefore, we are at the top of what ever God has created. God implies to us through scripture that there is no redemptive salvation for the angels who followed Satan.

Compelling events by men caused the Torah to become the Jewish sacred law (II Kings 22:8–20; II Chron. 34:15–24). Compulsion is the by product of many church by-laws today. Laws that stifle new observations. When we come the end of the Christian Church era, we find Jesus is forced to stand outside the church doors (Rev. 3:20). "And at that time shall Michael stand up, the great prince which standeth for the children of thy people: and there shall be a time of trouble, such as never was since there was a nation even to that same time: and at that time thy people shall be delivered, every one that shall be found written in the book. And many of them that sleep in the dust of the earth shall awake, some to everlasting life, and some to shame and everlasting contempt (Dan. 12:1–2).

Jesus came among His own back in the median of time, then was ostracized and put to death because of His nonconformity. Jesus presented a new way to look at the Old Testament in His day. The change was as drastic as what you are reading in this book. Of course He was infallible, when this book is not. That is why you should search the scriptures yourself.

Daniel preached about the end, but at the time he could not understand it (Dan. 12:8, 9). Some of his prophecy could not be fully understood until human history approaches the end and gives it a setting. Since we are approaching that time, we should now be able to look around us and recognize some signs (Matt. 24:43). All but one very important sign, and that would be the exact hour when the wrath of God is going to fall upon the Gentiles (Lu. 21:24). We will try to explain in our next chapter what these words mean.

What else grew on this earth while it was dark? What type of an atmosphere did the earth originally have? If God wanted animals to survive through this earth's darkened years, they would. Nine times in the first chapter of Genesis, we find the expression: "God said," and then it happens! The powers exercised in creating the universe allow God to change, redirect, or rearrange things. If

God did just renew the earth, there was no need to recreate everything. He could select at random some things used in the past. We
certainly cannot deny God that opportunity, not when Jesus could
call Lazarus back from the dead after four days.

God did not tell Noah to board fish on the ark. Why should
he? Fish do very well in water. Why then should God put a whole
new set of animals on the earth if He were only renewing it for
another human creation as stated in Ps. 104:30. Renewing the
earth for Adam was a modest endeavor compared to His original
creation from nothing. In Genesis, God creates from "yielding seed,
and the fruit tree yielding fruit after his kind, *whose seed is in itself,
upon this earth: and it was so*" (Gen. 1:11). Notice in Genesis how
each life form was commanded to multiply after its kind. This
sounds like a continuation of life rather than an original creation.
The original creation is found in Genesis 1:1 and Job 38:4–7.

After Adam and Eve, men have been creating themselves with
just a body and God's appointed soul in similitude with the animals. We differ from the animals because of our God like soul. It
remains eternal!

When Adam and Eve acted independently from God, they
stepped away from God's protective influence. As a result, they
became subjects, like animals, who can be manipulated and en-
ticed. Are ability to manipulate our human minds is connected to
God's spiritual attributes (Eph. 6:12). God is always there to help
us if we learn to abide be His spirit, but for us to grow, He leaves
us much to our own.

Man's fall happened when he was persuaded to misuse the gift
of freedom. Still, the high status of our soul, yearns for
independence. We just need to think before we act. Are we being

pulled or persuaded? Right thinking develops our individual character. Often we must go against our emotions. It is the devil who wants to kill our independence. His greatest asset is to use the persuasions of other men. He uses sickness and various other physical torments to make us get in lock step with one of his groups. To be alive with God gives us a limited degree of freedom and independence.

Pride is a luxury that only God can afford. He alone knows how to handle it. Pride in the human heart accomplishes false imaginations (See Jer. 3:17). False imaginations can ruin the human soul (See Ex. 20:5; Josh. 24:19; Na. 1:2; & II Cor. 11:2). God alone has the right to be jealous if He wants to be (See Ex. 20:5).

Pride and jealousy must be drained from men. Pride was the downfall of Satan. God tried to drive pride from man in Job's world through the fear of huge beasts. In our world He uses the buffeting by Satan. "For whom the Lord loveth he chasteneth, and scourgeth every son whom he receiveth" (Heb. 12:6).

ANGELS

Before the universe was ever formed, God created a host of angelic beings. At first they were called "morning Stars", or "Sons of God" (Job 38:7). The angels do predate the very existence of this earth, but they *were* created beings (Ez. 28:15). The angels and all things were created by God. It is God alone who stands outside of time! He resides in the "Beginning and the End" (Rev. 1:8).

Usage of the term "Sons of God" is not an Israelite expression. Scholars think the term must come from some old myths handed down prior to the call of God to Abraham. We know parts of the book of Genesis predated Abraham, yet the book of Genesis and the Book of Job, was assimilated into the Bible as true and factual. It is more natural for the Hebrew language to express "Sons of God" as plain 'gods' or just "mighty men". Angels still represent to us today as messengers and aid to men. What angels do to the naive is overwhelm them with something supernatural (Ps. 29:1). They are an entity that performs far beyond the human capacity.

After this earth was formed, there was a huge angelic rebellion in the spirit world. The Bible explains that this rebellion was under the direction and influence of Satan (2 pet. 2:4, Rev. 12:9— 12). Same people fail to realize this same rebellion continues until this very day. We as mortals find ourselves created right in the middle of this heavenly rebellion. It's harder for us to grasp the true significance of it because we are part of the physical underworld. Being made physical deprives us of the spiritual eyes to see all that's really going on. A huge disadvantage for us is that the spirit world can see us.

The Bible explains to us that some spirits rebelled over the disposition of men and rebelled against God. Being created in the underworld requires us mortals to develop the capabilities to identify source. To distinguish between the good source and the bad source. We are left quite alone to work this out. In the end we are expected to learn reasoning. To be able to think on our own rather than yeild to instincts. Lack of proper knowledge was the downfall of nations in the past (Hosea 4:6).

If you believe the Bible is a spiritual aid it will explain that Satan and his followers are confined to this earth (Is. Rev. 12:9). They are given power over the air (Eph. 2:2). This places them immune to earth's gravety. Be it good, or evil, there influences has an effect in developing our spiritual attitudes. Evil and good struggle with each other to influence our thoughts, and our thoughts control our bodies.

Satan possessed the body of the prince of Tyrus (Ez. 28:2). How many times he has influenced mortal men through others down through history is anyones guess. Satan can deceive by appearing to man in the form of an angelic being (2 Cor. 11:14). In a later chapter we shall describe an instance where Satan works through just one man to set up a group of otherwise wonderful people on earth that will develop to establish him as god in the last days. This group will aid Satan worldwide to become the great antichrist.

Hebrew 1:14 describe something enlightening about the good heavenly angels. Should God approve, good angels have the ability to appear and give us assistance when they choose. Many times their appearance goes unnoticed because they appear as a plain man or woman. This casual appearance is different from those whom God chooses to appear to men for a specific purpose. These angels speak in the first person. As with Hagar (Gen. 15:7), Abraham at the sacrifice of Isaac (Gen. 22:11), to Jacob (Gen. 31:13), at the burning bush (Ex. 3:2), and so on. Some angels have been named and personalized. Gabriel is an example in the book of Daniel.

Gabriel also appeared to Mary in the New Testament. Angels may approach us at grocery stores, airports, or anywhere there might be a personal distress. Some appearances with heavenly angles have gone quite unawares. Those who do become aware usually find out after the stranger who helps them simply disappears. Vanishes within the blink of an eye.

Angels are from the spirit world. A higher dimension. If we can obtain it we will judge these same angels at the white throne judgement (2 Cor. 6:3; Rev. 20:11). For now we are an important side issue. The real battle is being fought in heaven (Eph. 6:12). The results are, who among us is going to survive. It will be but a few (Mt. 7:14).

Our fallen state here parallels another dimension so close that its influence has a profound effect upon our souls. Evil spirits try to sway us one way, while good spirits try to sway us the other way. Paul tells us "That Christ may dwell in your hearts by faith" until we "may be able to comprehend with all saints what is the breadth, and length, and depth, and height; and to know the love of Christ, which passeth knowledge, that ye might be filled with the fullness of God" (Eph. 3:17-19). Notice how it is God who "passeth knowledge". This would be a SPIRITUAL knowledge,

because earthly knowledge is like vanity. It will one day just pass
away.

Bear in mind that the people of Job's semi-spiritual world were
not so corrupt as we mortals are. There was not the prodding of
Satan at first. Therefore their relationship with the physical was
much more divine than we have it today. They were able commune with the spiritual. When Adam and Eve fell they became
completely physical. Their first actions determine how they became sadly aware of the physical state. They became very uniquie
and quite mortal. They continued to live because of their souls,
but lacked the spiritual ingredient that sustains them for eternal
life.

Even light as we know it is restricted to the underworld. It has
limits to one hundred and eighty two thousand mile per second.
When light is broken down it is material. Spirits do not have a
vibrating ear drum in order to hear. Spirits communicate with
mental telepathy. We can go ahead and put out huge radio disks
but we are not going to hear anything from outside our world
unless it will be just plain static. We, In the state we are in, are
alone din the universe. All other object out there have spiritual
activity. We are the only place in the universe that has gone contrary to God. Bad spirits try to keep us bad, while the good spirits
try to teach us perfection. Think of it! If God abides in the physical it would take Him forever to traverse the universe. God did
become flesh. He too descended beneath all things (Heb. 2:9), so
that thoseworthy could also become perfect (Mt. 5:48).

We find in the Bible that Adam and Eve can not return again
to the spiritual on their own. Neither can any of their offspring.
This situation changed when God took upon Himself the flesh to

overcome that barrier. Now we are Justified by our faith (Rom. 5:1). From faith comes the thoughts we govern our lives by. This is how we find the spiritual (Jn. 4:24).

This earth was created to be inhabited by the underworld (Isa. 45:18). It is truly unique in the universe. Scientists are not going to receive any radio signals from out there because everything else in the universe is functioning on a spiritual level. Each planet and sun is filled with spiritual beings who are not on the bottom rung of the ladder as this world is. God did become flesh, and by doing so, He became the author of Salvation (Heb. 5:8,9). He descended beneath all things (Heb. 2:9), and came away perfect. Now we try to follow the example He left for us (Heb. 2:9).

Using the Bible rendition, we learn that Adam and Eve can not return to the spiritual world on their own. On the other hand, good angels, and Satan, have the ability to appear at will (I Cor. 11:14). Satan is very deceptive when he appears. He acts as though he was a messenger from God as he puts some diabolical scheme into effect.

Some humans have the ability to tap briefly into the spiritual world. In fact, we are all given premonitions. Everyone has heard of a friends special feelings that pompted them to avert disaster. Few have actual visions of things yet future. Unless directed by God the information they receive is garbled and mostly imprecise. Unauthorized visions can sometimes be so close to the facts it is amazing. A correct wild prediction can be misleading to those who have faith. The Bible warns us about false prophets and tells us we need to take heed of them (Mt. 24:24). For items spiritual we need to study the Bible and learn its genuine visions for the future. It has the explanation for eternal salvation and explains the final disposition of man.

There is the Apocrypha and other discourses that are informative to read. There are stories of the Baby Jesus while in Egypt. About Jesus as a young man in England and India. Such writings give you a broader base but add little to the Bible message.

We in turn we have an effect upon the spirit world by way we act. Naturally Satan's followers would rejoice for those among us who choose to do evil. Bad actions upon our part would drive away our protecting angels. Evil angels must flee from us when we do good (Js. 4:7). Evil angels are aghast at the sight of someone praying. There are many who will attest to the power of their prayers. Prayer has its effect because we live very close to a spiritual dimension. Jesus tells us that with Him we have life forever, while in the end, the wicked will perish (2 Pet. 2:10-21).

Since the world in general, and the churches in particular, are not aware there has been a mortal population on this earth before, they do not understand what is going on just beyond the limit of what we see, feel, and smell. There are objects in the sky made visible to us from time to time. It is hard for us to believe in them when we can see. The radar invention and other instruments have verified them and we still don't think they are there. Its been hard for us to accept the fact that something beside birds, bees, and butterflies can fly.

Lucifer was given full authority over Job and all the other mortals in that dominion (Job 1:12). We must realize Job's world was set both a mortal and spiritual relationship. This placed it far in advance of the world we live in today. When God and Satan quarreled, Job's world had to be eliminated. Many items remained intact to be used again in the future.

Isaiah is the first to describes that heavenly holocaust: Part of what he said is: "shall not be joined with them in burial" (Isa. 14:20). Satan and his angels did not join them in "burial." He and his followers were saved for events yet future. Restraints were put upon Satan and he was restricted to the confines of this earth until judgment day (Rev 12:9). Satan's dominion, Job and that mortal experiment, ceased at that time. The world became "without form and void." We can see the evidence of this holocaust in earth's own fossil record. Something terrible happened about sixty five million years ago.

For this increment in time all activity on earth slowed as it was put into a deep freeze. The earth was considered void because Gods spiritual kingdom did not function here. Satan was here when God blessed a portion of it for the Garden of Eden. At that time spiritual light came upon the earth. Satan's angels must have been delighted because before Eden there was little to do and no enlightening activities. They remembered a condition when this earth was frozen and feared it would happen again when talking to Jesus: "And, Behold, they cried out, saying, What have we to do with thee, Jesus, thou Son of God? art thou come to torment us before the time?" (Mt. 8:29).

Some experts agree after world war two the Russians and the United States modified their position towards each other because both came to realize we share a planet with someone else. Some one or something mystical with powers far beyond all that we know. Russia and the United States had little in common with each other but their own fear and hate for each other. They were ready to move on each other during the missile crisis of 1960. What really held them back was the fear of unidentified flying objects. One had crashed in the United States and another had crashed in Russia too. Both nations were aware of their vast technologies and the proof that we were not alone. Knowedge that ET,s were real tended to hold back a full nuclear exchange at the time. Why use them if some unknown enemy is poised to take over the world.

At loss to explain even their existence, governments have resorted to cover up, but at the same time they have been secretly investigating UFO,s for the past fifty years. Unable to explain UFO's has caused governments to deny they even exist. This flares in the face of about 3,000 personal sightings from people all over the world. Today there is a growing concern that crop circles are made by UFO,s. It does seem that these objects are just playing with us while all along they have awesome power that exceeds our earthly laws.

Technical advances brought about by World War Two, the airplane, radar. and the Atomic Bomb, made it easier to tell that there was indeed something our there that we knew nothing about. Since all research is secret, we are not being told that UFO,s have been in our skies since the beginning of time. Remembering the 1939 "War of the worlds" broadcast by Orsen Wells the nation was leery of letting a panic like that get started all over again. During the Second World War radar operators had observed peculiar objects with great speed, sharp impossible turns, then they would just disappear. They thought such sightings were a fluke of the radar scope because no object could perform in the air that way. To make a right angle turn in excess of five thousand miles per hour would create a "G" force that would crush a human into fluids. No one could possibly believe anything like this until one crashed outside Roswell New Mexico in July 1947.

Media attention that UFO,s did exist was very exciting news coming so close to the end of the war. This unusual news did bring out some mystics and kooks who claimed they had knowledge of the subject. Over time sightings have become to common that most people are conditioned to fact that strange things are happening on our skys. Some people claim they have been abducted and taken aboard. There have been cattle mutilations, and other strange happenings that suggest superior skills in order to perform. Since the UFO crashed at Roswell the government has been secretly studying its residue for years. For more than fifty years we have heard bits and pieces about UFO,s and how we have back engineered their technology. Today we find some of these men willing to talk and tell us the truth. Since UFO,s, and the back engineering projects remain a secret, these men are still consider kooks. Col. Philip J. Corso claims he was the second man in charge. He describes in his book "The Day After Roswell" that these Extraterrestrials were CLONED! Indeed he is correct! That's the reason these angels need spiritual vehicles to transport themselves. Why they can appear and disappear at will. They are part of the debris left over from the world of Job. Cloned anciently right here on earth? By a people of paradise ancestry that is now defunct?

Perhaps if Col. Corso had used the Bible along with his crash evidence he would have known that the ET,s he was dealing with are actually cloned angels made to do physical observations on earth prior to the time of Adam and Eve.

The UFO,s we see and hear about are a peculiar type of craft. They are able to materialize and de-materialize, just like regular

angels, in the blink of an eye. The Bible explains they were allowed to fraternize with the first women of this fallen human generation. The daughters of Adam and Eve (Gen. 6:1–8).

The Bible called them after their angelic spiritual description
"Sons of God." Being cloned, they are a special product, governed
by special directives. Being spiritually made they communicate by
mental telepathy. Those people who have been abducted by them
attest to that fact. Mental telepathy is a definite attribute of the
spirit world. In the spirit world there is no such thing as a lie.
Thoughts are wide open to be read by others.

Clones angels are programmed with certain instincts. They
were to put some spiritual attributes into the human race by breeding. The process failed badly. It produced Giants and other human digressions. It did accomplished added longevity to human
life. Men in those days lived for almost a a thousand years.

Fallen man is vile, vicious, and selfish. The killing of Abel by
Cain is evidence of man vial nature. God sought to improve man's
vile nature, by allowing the angelic clones to breed with them.
They being spiritual did lengthen the physical lives of men, but as
for jump starting the human race with spiritual inclinations, it
failed. Finally God was obligated to destroy that race, all but Noah
and his family. An alternative plan went into effect to save the
human situation. God Himself, would have to pay the price for
the redemption of men. God would make the sacrifice to instill
the spirit into man. Those whom God chooses to save will be
redeemed, and all others will perish along with Satan and his angelic
followers.

God often manipulates evil to gain His intended results. God though is separate from evil and is in no way responsible for it. Spiritual and moral evil arises from s dimple sinful attitude (Jas. 1:13-15). Men can do evil to the extent that it surprises God (Jer. 32:35). God blessed the children of Israel and tried to hold them as an example to all other nations. Again, this did not work.

Never-the-less a loving God respects all people in all nations and ethnic personalities. As individuals we need to find a spiritual balance that pleases God. Such a condition can be obtained by anyone. When our carnal mind is cultured to the spirit of eternal life that person is ripe to be adopted by God (Rom. Ch. 8).

Ezekiel was an apocryphal writer in the Old Testament. Some of the things he reveals are very hard at first to understand. After one has obtained knowledge of the broader view Ezekiel confirms the details. Ezekiel takes us through the tribulation period while the apocryphal writer John takes us on through Armageddon and the Millennia. Ezekiel describes what we know today as a UFO (Ez. Ch. 1). He describes it after the same manner many describe them today. They are indeed extra terrestrial because they are left over from Job's prior world here on this earth. To understand this is to know why there are footprints right along side with the dinosaur tracks. To accept that UFO's are of a heavenly origin explains many very puzzling questions about our own ancient past.

Hundreds of books have been written about UFO'S and many things have been attributed to them. Naturally there have been many hoaxes also because we are dealing with some new and mysterous force. We must realize that we are dealing with a residue of the spirit world. A spiritual being that has an instinct similar to that of our own worldly animals.

Some say that UFO'S can knock out electricity, others attribute crop circles to them. What is readily apparent is that they exceed our known technology. The Bible informs is that they did breed with the human race prior to the flood. Since that time they have been restricted from breeding, or otherwise inter mixing with mortals. They would still have sexual instincts and perhaps this is why they are so curious about reproductive organs. We must consider them to conduct themselves on instinct, similar to the animals we have in this world. To do a positive task they must be trained. Perhaps they transported early humans all over the world. Our earliest civilations show evidence to this effect. They may have helped to build Stonehedge, the pyramids, cities in the Americas, and even the building of Soloman's temple in Jerusalem.

After fifty years of knowing that they are out there, the world in general seems little disturbed about flying objects. They have become some kind of an oddity. People make movies about them. We joke about them. All because they are there and no one seems to know what they can do about it. Its true that they seem more of a pest than a threat. But up til now, no one has sxplained them. Neither has anyone tried to explain why people show up to help in dire situations and then just disappear. These are angels! Someone we share the planet earth with.

God said He would speed up His work in the last days: "But thou, O Daniel, shut up the words, and seal the book, even to the time of the end: many shall run to and fro, and knowledge shall be increased" (Dan.12:4). Yes, we are running to and fro because a flying saucer has crashed outside a small town of Roswell New Merico in the early morning hours July 1947. That crash should turn out to be the most significant story since the building of the pyramids in Egypt. Later the extraterrestial crash at Roswell was denied by the U. W. government. Yet, during the governmental denial technology springs forward at a fantastic pace. Items and residue from that crash site were quickly gathered up an turned over to industry for review. For fifty years it has helped us to advance our technologies in lasers, integrated circuitry, fiber-optics, night vision, and even the material for making bullet proof vests. These are a few items gleaned from space ship technology and done by the process of "reverse engineering". By examining the material found at the Roswell crash sight our scientists have learned how to use it. All this engineering has been kept secret because it was processed through countless military and civilian defense contractors. It was our government who financed the initial research and development.

At first the crash horrified our military because they thought it might be some Soviet secret weapon. It bore a resemblance to some German-designed aircraft like Jets and the flying wing. Not knowing what to do with it, and by not wanting to start another "War of the Worlds" panic, they covered it up. Over the last fifty years our government has examined the debris of this crash. Today the man who was placed in charge of the Roswell UFO crash has given an account of it in a book "The Day After Roswell—by Col. Philip J. Corso". Mr. Corso describes just how he was able to control a tremendous technological advances the united states has undergone during the last fifty years.

When Jesus was asked about His second coming, and what the end would be like, He expressly mentions Daniel: "When ye therefore shall see the abomination of desolation, spoken by Daniel the prophet (Mt. 24:15). Daniel's words include the ten kings, the antichrist, and the war that starts on Israel by a king to the south (Dan. 11:40). Daniel ask God about these these end time things and he was told they were sealed until people: "shall run to and fro." Daniel was not the only prophet to view end time events.

Most of the old biblical prophets had a glimpse into the end time era. Ezekiel was a prophet to see a flying saucer.

Ezekiel describes a flying saucer, and the 1947 crash at Roswell proves him right. At first our government admitted they hand a flying saucer. Then it was covered up. What is is interesting to know though was that the ET's riding the craft were killed. They lost their existence while being in their physical condition.

Bear in mind that these flying saucers were observed to disappear in flight! To go at speeds in access of 5000 miles per hour and then make a ninety degree turn. This would develop a "G" force that would crush humans. We must remember that these objects originated in Job's world. Job's world had a divine relationships with the physical world. These crafts were designed to swing back and fourth between the spiritual and the physical. Just like all other good, free thinking, and honest angels.

It is indeed shocking to know that these clones could die while in a physical state. Now we can understand why Satan was so interested in killing Jesus while He was yet physical. Satan took the chance that he could destroy Jesus while He was in the flesh (I Cor.2:7–8). The mystery Paul alludes to in these verses is that the divine nature of God is intra-dimensional. While physical, God still saw with spiritual eyes. Satan did not Understand the significance of this until after the resurrection when God became body, soul, and spirit. Satan is only soul and spirit. Cloned angels are spirit and body, and man is just soul and body.

Just imagine the potential of man. If we can become instilled with the spirit, we can share glory with God! A station in heaven where we judge angels (1 Cor. 6:3). If you want God's blessings go directly to HIS WORDS (Bible). You are blessed in the hearing of

God's words. Not by the words of this or any other book. The whole truth lays in God's word!

If you think the crash at Roswell was spectacular one can you imagine the effect flying saucers had on civilized man that pre dates the Old Testament? By the way in which they defy gravity it would have been a simple task for them to place megaton stones for people all over the world. Some thing we would have a hard time doing with our technology today. Why shouldn't these ancient nations get some angelic help? After all, Paul tells us that God is interested in all races and in all nations (Rom. 1:5).

In the America's the civilizations thrived briefly and then they fell into antiquity. On the other hand in Egypt the ancients maintained their society for thousands of years. God even allowed his promised people Israel to be cultured by the Egyptians. The Egyptian aspects remained strong so God Himself had to culture them about things spiritual while in the desert. From the strange happenings it in Exodus, UFO ships did some fly overs to distribute manna, etc. What puzzles us til this day is the ancients rock building technology. This tecnology exists all over the world. Just how did 120 ton stones ratchet themselves into their places. It is not hard to attribute this to ET's when we know they defy gravity to begin with.

The idea that there was another continent with high technology called Atlantis came first by an Egyptian. Plato picked up on the story and made it into a legend.

Over time God did succeed at developing the unused portion of the human brain until we retained the knowledge to live in the societies we live in today. With our world wide communications and accurate research we can now understand how the spiritual works.

The curse of Cain has been an enigma in the Bible. Even the scholars are puzzled over it. Cain is cursed to become a "fugitive and a vagabond" attached to this earth (Gen. 4:12) A fugitive places one outside of society, and a vagabond is listless, a wander, and a tramp. People lived to the age of nearly one thousand years in Cain's day, but his curse seems to endure much longer than that? Without UFO information we are left to think Cain did not survive Noah's flood?

On the other hand, if we accept flying saucers, Cain could have been taken up in one of them. Perhaps they are assigned to take Cain from place to place on earth. Is he Sasquatch, Big Foot, or the Yeti man? Those who have seen this ape like creature report that he is between seven and eight feet tall. There were "Giants" on earth in Cain's day (Gem 6:4).

Perhaps the mark on Cain is a real hairy body. Or mabye it is the skunk like odor he has about him? Our modern day Cain has the ability to disappear. Some people have seen him do just that. Others follow his tracks until they just disappear. It is recorded, that this human entity has been seen around for humdreds of years, yet no physical evidence of him have ever been found. Being a fugitive. Cain would be reluctant to contact any other human, and he remains obscure as the Bible directs. To be a vagabond Cain needs something like a space ship to get him around.

The spiritual aspects of the Bible will never be accepted by a carnal mind. The pragmatic and carnal mind will not accept miracles or anything supernatural, but Big foot and spacecraft have been seen by too many ordinary people to be just cast aside without any explanation. When things act like something from an-other world, its possible to come from another dimension in this one. Is It possible Cain disappears "in" that dimension for his promised protectkion (Gem. 4:14)? Do flying Saucers take Cain from one obscure place on the globe so he can be the vagabond the Bible describes? Is this why we can see evidence of him in Napal and sightings in Oregon USA. We need flying Saucers to give an explanation for some things in the Bible.

SATAN

The Book Of Job is truly a spiritual book by an unknown author. It occurs at a time when Satan exercised "power" over Job (Job 1:12). This fact alone makes it from another world. The argument we find there is the rift that exists between God and Satan. We miss the true substance of that argument if we fail to relate it to an existence that predates the creation of Adam and Eve. The argument between God and Satan was about God's compassion.

Since the people of Job were saved according to their own righteousness, Satan challenged the love of God, saying that it imperfect and blind. Satan felt that God was imperfect because he tended to favor those He loved. Man, being in the image of God, has a tendency to make the same error. We often favor one child over the other, those whom we like over others. Sometimes we make special allowances to those we love by automatic forgiveness in spite of who they are.

In our world today God demonstrates for all the true extent of His love and mercy. Had Satan known what we now know, he world never have allowed Jesus to be crucified (1 Cor. 2:8). By the way He died, God showed a perfect compasion, mercy, and love. Satan erroneously sought to take the throne of God because God was too weak in his mercy. God knew what He was doing, and now he uses Satan to make an even more perfect man.

The Book of Job tells us God created angels before He created the heavens and this earth (Job 38:4–7). According to Ezekiel chapter 28, Lucifer was once the most choice above all of God's angelic creation. But Lucifer came into rebellion. His rebellion caused him to become an enemy against God. As a result, God confined him, and the angels who consorted with him to this earth (Isa. 14:12; Rev. 12:9). Why choose this earth to confine Satan? Because it still his his dominion even though he made it "void" to God.

Revelation 12:9 tell us how Satan was limited to this earth. Now that he was cast out, Satan no longer has easy access to the heavens. He and his angels are confined here.

"Lucifer" in Hebrew means "son of the morning star." After his rebellion his name was changed to Satan, which means, "adversary" against God.

The Bible says Lucifer was once a "cherub that "covereth" (Ez. 28:14). A "cherub" is an angel (See Gen. 3:24). A "cherub that covereth" would describe an angel with dominion and authority. Jesus acknowledged Satan was in authority over earth when He called him "prince of this world" (Jn. 12:31; 14:30; 16:11).

When Jesus came into the world and lived the perfect life, Satan was judged (Jn. 16:11). This finished God's work on earth as he re-established His Spiritual kingdom. Not just a paradise, for now His Spirit co-exits on earth along with Satan's.

In the Old Testament God's Spirit was directed. Now that the

Holy Ghost resides on earth we can become somewhat immune to the devil (Jas. 4:7). The period man now lives in is more appropriately called "Grace". Some who opt for the spirit will not taste death in the last days (I Cor. 15:52). Those who opt for evil will in the end find the earth "swept and garnished" (Lu. 11:25). It will melt by fire (II Peter 3:10).

Satan was *not* with God at the *very* beginning. He was among the *angelic* creation (Ez. 28:15). Jesus on the other hand, *was* with God from the beginning (Jn. 1:1–5).

It is true that we have Satan walking around heaven in the first chapter of Job, but at that time, Satan had every right to be with God. He was not confined to this earth yet. Satan's decision to oppose God caused the earth to be covered by darkness and Satan's works therein were "void" to God.

Job 1 and 2 leave us with ample reason why there became a rift between God and Satan. He became very jealous of man! Perhaps he learned that men's final destiny was to become higher than the angels (See 1 Cor. 6:3). The Bible explains: "thou was perfect in thy ways from the day that thou wast created, till iniquity was found in thee" (Ez.28:15).

Paul tells us we do not wrestle against flesh and blood, but against heavenly principalities (Eph. 6:12). Paul is talking about fallen angels who continue the struggle over what God intends for man. Satan is a spiritual being who wrestles for the domination of our souls. His ways are very habitual and compelling. He was a murderer from the beginning and the father of all lies (Jn. 8:44).

When Lucifer ruled man in Job's world he favored the man to be compelled rather than to be free. A dictatorship is the best form of government, but there has to be a benevolent leader. Satan was not that person.

Satan can be limited by man (I Cor. 10:13; Eph. 6:11). Satan is very cunning, and his ways may not always be obviously evil. On occasion he may be used by God to set forward the cause of right (I Cor. 5:5; II Cor. 12:7). God used Satan in the garden when he said to Eve: "For God doth know that in the day ye eat thereof, then your eyes shall be opened, and ye shall be as gods, knowing good and evil" (Gen. 3:5). Acting upon their own did make Eve independent, but the consequence of her independence brought shame and physical death. The lie Satan told Eve was, "Ye shall not surely die" (Gen. 3:4). Eve died a spiritual death as the spirit of God left her. Adam followed her, and they both experienced shame, as they became subject to the desires of the flesh. To grow old, suffer, and die. But God had a plan of redemption for man, and He assured Eve she would be redeemed (Gen. 3:15).

Adam and Eve were now forbidden to partake of the tree of life lest the remain forever in their physical state. (Gen. 3:24). Now this presents a paradox. Just how is God able to keep His first promise to Eve. The paradox is, that mercy could not take effect lest it destroy justice. So God has prepared this earth as a probationary state before rendering judgement upon man. In man's probationary state there is time for repentance. The plan of mercy could not be brought about except an atonement be made. Thus God Himself atoned for the sins of the world. The atonement was necessary so that God might be a perfect and a just God also. Thus, Inadvertently, God used sin to create a better man. A man who knows sin, but is willing to opt out of it.

To this end, God admits He "creates" evil (Isa. 45:7), and in the same verse, God also admits that it is He who "creates the "darkness" also. God simply creates everything!

When God said, "Let there be light," in Genesis 1:3, but the sun did not automatically turn on. In fact, the sun does not appear for three more days. At this first instant, God illuminated the earth with spiritual light! The power of the Holy Ghost was set in motion. The sun was actually here from the first creation, but it did not start to shine until God relieved the earth from its darkened state.

The Genesis account is a simple re-creation of our earth to accommodate a new human race. Satan remained here when God put the world into darkness. He was not permitted to approach God's paradise called "Eden" without the aid of an animal.

The advantage men have over Satan is our redemption. Man has the ability to develop an immunity to Satan's power by learning to follow in the truth of God's light. No where in the Bible does it say fallen angles are redeemed.

Adam and Eve were created after the image of God. They were given a soul that is everlasting. Being made in the image of God gave man a soul of immense power. It is ever lasting but incomplete until it connects with the spirit. Be it the spirit of God, or of the devil. This is our option.

The scriptures show that men's freedom to choose is very revered by God and His angels. Most of us are awake to these facts.

We can forever remain in darkness (cut off from the glorious presence of God), or our souls may be redeemed by God. The choice us up to us and we will be judged by our own course of action.

We inherit the sin condition from our first parents in the garden of Eden. Our physical life on earth became a place for probation. At judgement day God will judge the attitude and character of all people (Rom. 9:15).

So it is up to us to develop our minds to reject evil and choose the good. We learn: "Precept upon precept; line upon line" (Isa. 28:10). The only way we can understand spirituality is to think things through. Many of us are too lazy to think on our own. Yet it is requested: "prove all things; hold fast that which is good" (I Thes. 5:21).

Where is our justice? It is not our fault we are born into this world dominated by Satan. God told Eve that He was going to fix things. He would do it through the "seed" of woman (Gen. 3:15). God kept that promise to Eve when He entered this world through woman's womb. God became flesh, and lived to the age of thirty exactly as you or me. He came into this world to Judge Satan and atone for the sins of men.

When He was bestowed with the Holy Ghost He became God personified in the flesh (Col. 2:9). We understand this the way He spoke with supreme authority during his ministry.

Satan brought judgment upon him and his followers when he persuaded others to kill Jesus (1 Cor. 2:7,8). Otherwise God would have lived forever in the flesh. Jesus voluntary took the sins of others in order for Him to die. God was predestined to do this act before the second creation began.

This benevolent act broke down the wall of partition between God and men (Ep. 2:14), thus making it possible for each of us to become priests and kings (Rev. 5:10) in the world to come.

God's presence is now on earth in the form of the Holy Spirit (Acts 2). He shines on earth through thoughtful and believing men (I Jn. 4:4). The Holy Ghost will remain until the times of the Gentiles are fulfilled. At that moment He will lift from earth, taking with Him all those thoughtful and believing people (II Thes. 2:7). When it leaves, many restraints will be lifted from Satan, and the world will go into seven more very turbulent years.

Satan may have thought he was succesful when he caused the scattering of the ten tribes of Israel back in 721 B.C. The devil has lost track of the ten tribes, but God knows where they are (Ez. 34:13–16). They play a very important part in God's future plans (Isa. 29:14; more later). The blood of lost Israel has become mixed among the Gentiles.

During God's current period of grace, those with a strong concentration of Israelite blood, may respond to God's gospel wherever they may encounter it. They are wheat among the tares (Mt. 13:25). When they respond to the gospel it often causes family problems: "The father shall be divided against the son, and the son against the father; the mother against the daughter, and the daughter against the mother; the motherin law against her daughter-in-law, and the daughter in-law against her mother in-law (Lu. 12:53), "And a man's foes shall be they of his own household" (Mt. 10:36).

Peter tells us how confused Satan will be under grace: "Be sober, be vigilant; because your adversary the devil, as a roaring lion, walketh about, seeking whom he may devour" (I Pet. 5:8). He tries to dissuade those who respond to the thruth. So, when a sinner does make a spiritual connection with God, they can expect a rash of trouble. It is the sinner who seems to have smooth sailing and earthly gains. People who you once admired may turn out to be your most avid foe. Never-the-less, praise God for your chastisement: "For whom the Lord loveth he chasteneth, and scourgeth every son whom he receiveth" (Heb. 12:6). Just think about how the first apostles were scourged to put to death.

One of Satan's best beguiling tools is to mesmerize people into thinking as a group. This activity does not connect to the independent thoughts of Jesus as He set His example for others to follow. One should come to God as an individual, and by their own volition.

Being good serves God more than a million words, but let that which come out of the mouth be "edifying, that it may minister grace unto the hearers (Eph. 4:29). Before you believe, it is up to you to "prove all things" to yourself.

Church group association is very effective, the way they introduce you to God, but they often fail when it comes to dispensing knowledge (Rom. 10:2–3). Much can be gleaned from churches, but one is better off to choose a church group who is open to independent thought In our world today, Satan is using modern psychology: "Think hard enough and it will happen." Many churches have adopted this standard.

Satan has found a way to misdirect the truth in some churches simple because they try not to offend anyone. That they can not explain they leave to faith. Their reference to faith however, often avoids pure and simple logic. We ourselves must identify God personally if we are to have "eternal" salvation (Jn. 17:3). That means separating with logic the function of the Father from the Son in spiritual terms (II Tim. 4:3–4).

The Bible is abundant with stories portraying how God turned evil situations into good. Genesis chapter 38, Ester, and Jacob are an example of this. Regardless of how close to God men are, Satan does some of his best works (I Cor. 7:5). We read of his work in a professed believer called Ananias (Acts 5:3). Satan hinders the work of missionaries (I Thes. 2:18). He takes away the spirit sown in abiding hearts of men (Mk. 4:15), and his activity can produce physical effects (Lu. 13:16). Too many fine Christian young men and women have a "zeal of God, but not according to knowledge" (Rom. 10:2). It is easy to see why blind faith is insufficient, so we are advised to put on the whole armour of God (Eph. 6:11).

God was forever been a mystery to Satan. There is hidden wisdom that made Satan unaware of what God was up to when He came into Satan's domain. "Which none of the princes of this world know: for had they known it, they would not have crucified the Lord of glory" (I Cor. 2:8). The worldly appearance of God puzzled Satan as Jesus did conquered death. A proformance that destroyed the hold Satan had over man (I Jn.3:8; Heb. 2:14).

The Bible leaves no doubt as to the severity of the contest. Peter stresses the ferociousness of the battle as he describes him as a "roaring lion" (I Peter 5:8). Paul explaination is that he is very "cunning." In the end, Jesus shall prepare a refiners fire for the earth (Mt. 25:41), and Revelations 20:10 tells when that fire comes to pass. It is interesting to note, that this fire Peter describes in II Peter 3:10, does not occur until the final judgement day.

Lets go back to Paul and review how Satan has the power to appear as an "angel of light" (II Cor. 11:14). Imagine the excitement that would accompany such a spectacular event. Look at what happened after Mohammed supposed visit by the angel Gabriel. Sacred scripture was made available and a new religion was established. Another similar appearance can be found in the United States. The end result was another religion and their sacred Book of Mormon.

The Mormon's claim there founder, Joseph Smith Jr, had a vision depicting both the Father and the Son at the same time! This vision is attributed to Joseph Smith after his death. If the event is genuine, it destroys the basic theme of the Bible. Such a vision proposes many Gods; a theme that Satan has tried to put across every since he talked to Eve. Are men so spiritually deprived they separate the Father from the Son? Are we now still as dumb as Eve?

Wars, bad accidents, birth defects, sickness, moral abuse, and cultish religions are tools used by Satan. Men's willingness to sin in the past can cause hereditary defects to be passed on for generations (Ex. 20:5). The devil has been very cunning to develope these two new religions. Each one has become very effective. Mohammedism to withstand the spread of Christianity, and Mormonism to counterfeit it in the last days.

Both of these new faiths claim the Bible as unreliable. The Book of Mormon claims the Indians are Jews and Jesus came to them those three days His body laid in the tomb. Both religions wind up exalting man to a God status. In 612 BC, there was words added to the Bible by wicked priests. This act caused God to turn away from Israel (Rom. 11:8–15). By altering the Bible and stoning the prophets, Isreal became oblivious to the fact that their Messiah would come among them first as a servant (Isa. Ch. 42).

According to the Bible, Christianity will digress in the days (Mt. 24:37). The success of Mormonism confirms this. We will wain in knowledge until we become like Noah's time.

God promised us through Amos the prophet that He will do nothing unless "he revealeth his secret unto his servants the prophets" (Amos 3:7). If you are attached to a church that neglects to inform you about the future, you are in a church that lacks spiritual guidance. You may as well become a Mormon, because they have a whale of a tale about the last days, and for sinister reasons. Studying the Bible is your best bet for understanding the future. God's plan is there.

Learn who is speaking, and when it is God's edict. Not all the words recorded in the Bible came from God. God did not tell Abraham to take Hagar to become his wife. Sarah is responsible for this act. God certainly did not tell Moses to kill the Egyptian. He did it on his own. The Bible carries many frailties of human nature, but it also contains what God has in store for man. So the Bible must be read in context, and from start to finish, before the truth is known.

God even puts information in the Bible that could not become known until the Bible was published en masse. This is a promise to those who earnestly read it all the way through: "no one of these shall fail…" (See Isa. 34:16). Right and wrong are clearly defined if one will take the time to disseminate it by reading the Bible all the way through. The Bible is formulated to develop your spiritual minds.

Jesus said the true believer may recognize the signs that pertain to the last days (Mt. 24:43). All one has to do is put biblical prophecy into its logical order. The Jewish return to Jerusalem to form their nation begins "that" final generation the Bible speaks about. Yes, there are people to be alive in "that" generation when the end comes. Since that time the Jews have trickled back from all over the world, and world events will come to make Jews flood back to Jerusalem.

Jesus promised the believer: "he will shew you things to come" (Jn. 16:13). Those who tell you that end time prophesy is mysterious and confusing are not familiar with their Bible. At the very lest they are overlooking the prophesies recorded in the Old Testament. Truths many people through the ages have died for.

Righteous indignation, along with ignorance, are not the attributes of God. Common sense should tell you this.

The Bible tells us faith by itself is dead (Jas. 2:24), just as the "body without the spirit is dead" (Jas. 2:26). Most Christian churches talk about Jesus, yet they do not explain Him. Instead, they leave him standing outside their doors (Rev. 3:20). Jesus is still trying to work with today's churches. He describes the end time church era as "Laodicea." Those who will find Jesus in this difficult church era will find a place with Him and His Father in heaven (Rev. 3:21).

Satan's favorite ploy is to mesmerize humanity until none dare question, or attempt to raise an original thought. Satan herds the unsuspecting into groups where the thought provisions are made for the many by a few at the top. Those in the group take comfort from being part of the many. *What the many believe*, they think, *must be true*.

We do not need the advice of others to resist the devil (Jas. 4:7), not when we have God's word as our standard. "Therefore it is no great thing if his minister also be transformed as the ministers of righteousness; whose end shall be according to their works" (II Cor. 11:15). We have seen some work these ministers do on our national TV. Their tongues seem golden, the way they teach fables in the name of Jesus Christ. Though some are found out, others step up to replace them. As long as men are willing to be deceived, Satan will provide ministers of deception.

One's own self-serving heart (soul) can become their worst enemy (Jer. 3:17). Satan works within men's soul to make one feel good inside. This self inflicted warming happens when one feels good about themselves for a variety of reasons. True faith on the other hand, must be supplemented by wisdom enough to stand in awe of His eternal greatness (Eph. 3:19).

The stronger "church first" organizations will massage human egos until they feel a strong burning in their bosoms. Love of oneself is the beguiling tool of Satan. Some churches encourage their members to rely on their burning in their bosom sensations. This burning in the bosom experience has much in common with our modern day psychology. The power of suggestion plays a major role in people's responses and reactions. Some doctors say that the greater percentage of most illnesses come from what the patient puts into his own mind. "Think hard, and it will happen." When it does not happen, the prognosticators who espouse this method will reverse the guilt from themselves by saying one is not concentrating hard enough.

The burning in the bosom desire is what motivates the thief and the murderer. Their excuse when caught is to say that something inside them made them do it. Now that psychology has made its way into the courtrooms of our justice system, intelligent men are buying the notion that their clients are not responsible. It is someone else's fault that the criminal did what he did. They say the fault lies with his abusive father, mother, or one may be racially frustrated. Some are now blaming state and local governments for not providing the proper information and care.

Quite opposed to these feelings is a spiritual encounter with God. This causes your inner soul to take on its own personal responsibility. A responsibility that senses truth and abides by it. One usually remembers when such a miracle takes place, but if not exercised and maintained, Satan can slide you into his burning in the bosom trap. The correct spirit must be continually cultured by genuine spiritual knowledge in order for it to continue (Rom. 10:2). The Bible explains, if one does not continue to fill their spiritual lamp, it may go out (See Mt. 25).

In later chapters we will learn how desperate Satan becomes as he tries to set himself up to be higher on this earth than Jesus. Once the restraining power of the Holy Ghost leaves this earth, Satan is going to try and impress men that it is *he* who has power over the resurrection. Through a surrogate, Satan is going to raise from the dead (Rev. 13:3). He comes alive as a mortal by his healing power (Rev. 13:2). Such a spectacular event is going to deceive many alive in this world who still do not understand the true resurrection of Jesus. Satan will rule forcefully during those evil times when he masquerades as God. Satan will sanction this spectacular event by declaring himself to be god in the Jewish temple (Mt. 24:21; II Tim. 2:4).

Except for one thousand years when he is bound, we have not seen the end of Satan's activities yet. How some of his activities fits in will become evident as we proceed on with the next chapters.

JESUS

"Ye are from beneath; I am from above" (Jn. 8:23).

By saying these words Jesus draws a distinction between Himself and we mortals. Men are conceive here on earth, but Jesus was not. "Thou bearest record of thyself; thy record is not true" (Jn. 8:13). "Ye neither know me, nor my Father: if ye had known me, ye should have known my Father also" (Jn. 8:19)

It is very sad, but as Christianity drifts further from the knowledge of their God, they further deny any spiritual understanding of His divine nature. We must rely our individual self to discern the spiritual events Jesus presented to us. Jesus explains, and Bible records it. Though flesh, Jesus is unique. Physically He was a "*eunuch*" (Mt. 19:12)! After the Holy Ghost fell He could see the spirit world and read the mental thought of other mortal men.

"And God said, Let *us* make man in our image, after our likeness" (Gen. 1:26). These words were spoken to Adam before Eve was separated from his body. So Adam too, was first in the image of God! Adam at first, was created both "Male and female" (Gen. 2:7)! Eve was extracted from Adam later (Gen. 2:21, 22). Now apply all this to what Jesus was saying.

If Jesus was both the Father and the Son (Jn 10:30), He would display a mortal body similar to Adam's before there was a sexual differentiation. If Jesus were not corrupt He would indeed be a eunuch. Genesis belabored the subject that Eve became separated from Adam. Perhaps so after they fell, they could reproduce themselves in the flesh. We are also told in scripture, that all shall be resurrected as eunuchs (Mt. 19:12), "for the kingdom of heavens sake." Jesus also says in this same verse: "He that is able to receive it, let him receive it." One seldom hears a sermon upon this subject, but it is gospel.

It makes little difference to God whether we be male or or female while in our physical existence. It is our immortal spirit that is being cultured and developed. Our flesh bodies are just temporary! Designed to procreate while here on earth. In this respect, Jesus is minutely different from you or me. Jesus was making it very clear that we would not be recognized by our sex organs in heaven.

As we dwell upon this earth, God is preparing a new place in heaven for us (Jn. 14:2, 3). Having bodies like his will eliminate our earthly appetite for sex and replace it with the Holy Ghost. In our heavenly dominion we will take upon the nature of holy angels (Lu. 20:34–36). Our end shall be to judge angels (I Cor. 6:3).

Jesus, as God, could have appeared on earth as a man. In the same manner that He did to Jacob (Gen. 32:24:28; 35:9–10). He could have appeared as a toddler, a teenager, or walked upon the world scene under circumstances other than what he did. Rather, He came in a manner that would leave man without any excuse. The Holy Ghost took over Mary's womb and preformed he transformation of God into the flesh. God at first was born as we are.

Grew up as we do, so that we can not say: "You do not know what it was like to be young."

Jesus was also different from men because the flesh of men inherits corruption (1 Cor. 15:42, 43). Jesus did not inherit corruption because of His immaculate conception. In every way, He remained immaculate. When Jesus received the Holy Ghost He was able to see the spirit world as plain as He was able to see the physical world. He addressed them on contact, and He had a mental confrontation with Satan.

Study the attributes of Jesus. Take into consideration some of the miracles He preformed an pay specific attention to some of the things He said. He received all the power of the Holy Ghost, but cloaked His glory within the flesh. The way Jesus performs make it impossible for one to announce

His name and declare themselves saved on a certain date. they were not saved, they merely felt His presence for the first time. They are not promised eternity until they learn to follow Jesus through to His death and resurrection.

Down through the ages we have learned the art of paying lip service to biblical doctrine without thinking about what the scripture really says. This allowes erroneous churches, like the Utah Mormons, to get away with counterfeiting, and pretending to be "Christian." Mormons believe in three separate and *distinct* Gods, who agree in one purpose. Lacking the real message of God has made the churches compete for a believers zeal only (See Rom. 10:2). The sad part of it is, the Mormon Church out race them all when it appeals to zeal only teachings. Their appeal is to reduce Jesus to where He is no more than their elder brother.

Eternal life is *assured* once you gain the *knowledge* of God: "And this is life eternal, that they might know thee the only true God, and Jesus Christ, whom thou has sent" (Jn. 17:3). This scripture marks the difference between the Old and New Testaments. In the Old Testament one worshipped by faith alone. Wisdom to gain spiritual knowledge came through prophets, priests, and some benevolent kings in the Old Testaments. With the advent of Jesus this all changed. We now have the example of our God in the flesh. Under God's grace we can now be assured by knowing.

Faith, and knowledge, turn into a wisdom of Him. Through wisdom we know whether we are doing right or wrong. Jesus did not inherit the sin condition, but rather He subjected Himself to it voluntary, knowing that He would overcome. He knew what was to happen to Him in order for Him to die a mortals death. Mortals may be able to follow Him by understanding the events that involve His resurrection.

Though they offered sacrifice by proxy, few understood its direct physical association of God in the Old Testament. The priests lost its proxy message. God remained a mystery until He did come to earth and undertook the personnel sacrifice: "And being made perfect, he became the author of eternal salvation unto all them that obey him" (Heb. 5:9). How was He made perfect? By overcoming death of the flesh.

Before God came into this world His Spirit did not blanket all of the earth. It was directed through those who God chose to speak. Usually they were wise men, prophets, or priests. After conquering Satan, Jesus was able to return the spirit to the earth as a "Comforter" (Jn. 14:16). We no longer need a mortal priest to advise us because we have a priest "who has passed into heaven" (Heb. 4:14–16).

Faith alone, in the Old Testament, could not give God a name. In the New Testament, we start by knowing His name, then try to give Him no more than a masculine existence. We must understand His conception, death, and resurrection.

Jesus is the very Eternal Father (See Jn. 10:30; (13: 10–11). "The mighty God, the everlasting Father, the Prince of Peace" (Isa. 9:6). Jesus, in the flesh, became both our Father and the Son. The Son because He subjected the flesh to the will of the Father, being both the Father and the Son, gave the Son (Flesh) victory over death, and make intercession for the children of men. Jesus is the Old Testament "I Am," Jehovah, or "Yahweh," God rolled into one. Jesus is the name given for God's flesh. Jesus is also the Creator of all things as He became the spoken "Word" in the flesh (Jn. 1:1–11).

God, performing in the flesh, fills messianic prophecy by Daniel, who refers to him as "Son of Man" (Dan. 7:13–14). No doubt Daniel was aware of what his role would be. The Messiah came to earth and rendered himself to be the servant of men, a role prophesied many times over by the prophets of old.

To appease sin, God obligated Himself to come to earth and fix it, but mercy cannot rob justice. For God to be a merciful and a just God also, He must render himself to the flesh. For the first time since the garden of Eden, God's Spirit came to dwell on this earth when it was manifested to Jesus after He was baptized by John (Jn. 1:33). After Jesus died, His kingdom, or that spirit remained on earth with us (Jn. 16:7). This is good news. This is why today we pray, rather than do sacrifice.

It is not really our fault we are born into a sinful world. That is why our merciful God has condescended to men. God fixed the problem. He conquered death, but it all stops there. Mercy does not rob justice, because we have to justify ourselves before we may enter God's kingdom. Please understand that a single God entity preformed as Jesus did.

Adam and Eve, or for that matter, all males and females inherit the sin condition. All, that is, but one. God came into this world being fashioned by the Holy Ghost (Mt. 1:18). Some perceive this as an immaculate conception, but exactly how Jesus was conceived is not known. Never-the-less He was formed in the womb of woman after the manner of any other mortal child. Just exactly like it was prophesied. Jesus was the "Immanuel" spoken of in Isaiah 7:14–16.

"Immanuel" in Hebrew means "with us is God." After Jesus received the Holy Ghost, He did miracles and other Godly acts while in the flesh. Unlike the prophets of the Old Testament, who spoke with *delegated* authority, Jesus spoke with direct, divine, and *supreme* authority. God, in human flesh, fulfills God's first great promise to humanity He made to Eve (Gen. 3:15). A promise to take away Satan's ability to hold men in death because their sins.

Until read with spiritual eyes some impressions in the Bible can be very confusing (See Jn. 4:24). "For it is written, he taketh the wise in their own craftiness" (I Cor. 3:19). Natural men are weak and have a tendency to lose sight of God. People do not like to hear the unusual, but rather they like to hear fables that tickle their ears. (II Tim. 4:3–4). Every man's soul has a certain void that leaves us unfulfilled and wanting. In times past men have invented rock gods to fill this void. Under New Testament grace we can fill the void with the Spirit of Christ.

Study the death of Jesus realizing that His soul is the Father. Then understand in order to be saved you must become three within yourself (I Thes. 5:23). You have to receive God's kingdom (spiritual nature) in order to be saved. God is not going to save anyone against His will.

Just how *did* God lay down his mortal life and still live? To answer that question we first must perceive God as an *intradimensional* being! Certainly men do *not* have the ability to rise from the dead without some help. It is by God's mercy that we are pulled from our sinful condition.

When we die, we become suspended souls, heavenly beings who must orient their souls to the spiritual world. Some will return for their bodies to dwell with God on earth for one thousand years. Some will be changed for this event when they are caught up to meet Christ on his return (1 Cor. 15:51, 52). The unredeemed ones will remain suspended through this same thousand-year period, and then they meet Jesus for the final judgment (Rev. 20:11).

By becoming knowledgale of the resurrection of Jesus, we can get a glimpse of what God's kingdom may be like. It involves knowing the way Jesus died and how He could rise from the dead. This makes us familiar about how the Holy Ghost functions to begin the human life of Jesus, and what part He plays in His death. God shows a lot of mercy towards man and He had a way or doing it without robbing justice. Know these things and the truth shall set us free (Jn. 8:32).

When God became a man, He placed himself below his own angels, only because He became an infant child: "But we see Jesus, who was made a little lower than the angels for the suffering of death, crowned with glory and honour; that he by the grace of God should taste death for every person" (Heb. 2:9). Jesus shared with all men physical pain and the emotional anxieties involved with growing to maturity. God's mortal life gives us all a spiritual map to show a way to be redeemed (Heb. 5:8,9). Jesus was the first person to rise from the dead (Phil. 3:10).

Satan and his angelic hosts did not understand why God came into this world until after they arranged to have Him killed (See 2 Cor. 2:7–8). They knew who Jesus was, but they thought God was inclined to appreciate this world (Mt.1:8–9), rather than pass judgement on the demons.

Where does one acquire this spiritual discernment? From learning through spiritual eyes as they read God's words and commune directly with Him. As each person is different, ones prospective may vary. The test is not to let other men intimidate or inhibit you. Remain open for God's promptings.

It takes a sincere and determined seeker of God to tap into spiritual matters. First you gain the thought, then your thought is confirmed by scripture. Others can excite a zeal for you, but a greater excitement comes when you see God at work arranging your thoughts. Under God's guidance one is given to know the greater mysteries. Most of all the Bible teaches the tragedy of what happens to nations and kingdoms when men listen to other men rather than to God.

Brilliant men try to rank Jesus among the famous philosophers of the past. They compare Him to men like Buddha, Mohammed, and Confucius. This way they can neatly categorize Jesus without confronting the real issue of His life. Was Jesus actually God as He claimed? Did Jesus indeed come back from the dead? World scholars like to avoid such questions, yet the facts surrounding the death and resurrection of Jesus are the most verifiable in recorded history. As historical records go, there are more than 3000 people who independently speak of the resurrection.

Sixteen Roman guards, plus an unknown number of regular temple guards, were able to attest to the fact that the dead body of Jesus vanished from His tomb. Thousands confirm that He dwelt among men for another 40 days. Still others witness Him ascending into the heavens (Acts 1:9). The wisdom of men does diminish when confronted by the astounding facts about Jesus. A proper analysis of the subject would tend to draw the honest in heart to accept Jesus as God. Either Jesus was Who He said He was (Jn. 10:30), or He is the biggest fraud ever to be perpetrated upon this earth.

Jesus left no personal writings. There are no original statues, monuments, or other memorabilia. Still His brief presence on earth has impacted it more than any other event in history. After all the miracles He performed, He asked His followers to judge Him according to one sign. He said He would come back and retrieve His body. God realized how Satan can duplicate many miracles, so he asked us to stake are faith on one Satan could not duplicate.

The enemies of Jesus knew what He said about coming back for his body (Mt. 27:63). When an angel rolled back the stone of His tomb, they tried to bribe the guards to say the body was

whisked away by a zealous follower (Mt. 28:12–13). These guard-
ing Jesus became witness to His resurrection! They were independent as they cried through the streets of Jerusalem what they saw.

"An evil and adulterous generation seeketh after a sign; and
there shall no sign be given it, but the sign of the prophet Jonas.
For as three days, and three nights in the whale's belly; so shall the
Son of man be three days and three nights in the heart of the
earth" (Mt. 12:39–40). In simple terms, Jesus was asking His followers not to believe a word He said if He did not come back and
retrieve His own physical body. It was done before many witnesses
and after a fashion His worst enemies could not deny.

Demons are known to possess living bodies who claim they
are from the past, but no one has remained in the grave for three
days, and then retrieved their physical body since Jesus. In a later
chapter we show how satan counterfeits it.

Jesus had power over His own life and death: "No man taketh
it from me. I have power to lay it down, and I have power to take
it up again. This commandment have I received of my Father" (Jn.
10:18). And who is the Father? The living soul dwelling within
Jesus (Jn. 13:10; Ez. 18:4)!

Jesus became the blood sacrifice as symbolized in the Old Testament (See 1 Cor. 5:7). Jesus is our chief priest to identify with,
"forever" (Heb. 5:6).

He replaced the Old Testament symbol of circumcision with
baptism, saying: "…it becometh us to fulfill all righteousness"

(Mt. 3:15). Baptism becomes the physical manifestation of our desire to repent and follow Jesus. It shows our willingness to en-join with the manifest spirit of Jesus which has the power to wash our sins away.

Sin did not have a place in the material body of Jesus. Therefore, baptism was only a symbolic for Him, proving that the act in itself does not save. The manifest of the Spirit saves. Baptism just demonstrates a willing heart. A spiritual yearning to be fed the spiritual truths of knowledge.

Jesus acknowledged baptism as a physical act of willful repen-tance. His own baptism demonstrated a physical desire for closer spiritual association. This demonstration brought Jesus to the apex where the spirit entered into him. Now he is able to see both the *spirit world along with the physical*. The Holy GHost now constantly remained with Jesus for the rest of His mortal life (Jn. 1:33). Jesus commanded the Spirit to leave Him at the end so he could die a human death (Lu. 23:46). Yes, Jesus laid down His own life, bodily.

The heavens lit up when the Holy Ghost fell upon Jesus in the form of a dove. All those present had their minds pierced by a voice saying: "This is my beloved Son, in whom I am well pleased" (Mt. 3:17; Mark 1:11; Lu. 3:22). This event unites the Holy Ghost with the body and soul of Jesus. At that very moment, Jesus is ren-dered "God personified in the flesh" (Col. 1:9). Jesus became Deity in the flesh.

We know from scripture that while Jesus was growing up He had a inquisitive mind. When He was very young, Jesus was able to confound the doctors with his knowledge of spiritual things

(Lu. 2:46–50). Other scripture suggests his body had human passions. He wept, and He could be moved to anger.

After receiving the Holy Ghost, He functioned as God! Forgiving sins and speaking with authority. He now *command the elements* as all heavenly power was vested in Him. Indeed, from that moment on, Jesus had to be careful how He spoke. He did forgive, but now He was very careful not to condemn. God knew that from His word alone came eternal happenings.

Once Jesus condemned a fig tree by saying: "Let no fruit grow on thee henceforward for ever. And presently the fig tree withered away" (Mt. 21:19). One word of condemnation upon his detractors who mocked Jesus at His trial would have spontaneously snuffed out the lives of those accusing Him, just as surely as He snuffed out the life of the fig tree.

After the spirit fell upon Jesus, He started his ministry (See Lu. 4:18–24). Jesus had to dismantle the Deity in order to die. First, the Father left Jesus by the shedding of His blood. Thus, he *poured* out his *soul* with his blood (Isa. 53:12). "For it is the blood that maketh an atonement for the soul" (Lev. 17:11). This is what the Old Testament Sacrifice tried to symbolize. "For the life of the flesh is in the blood." The Savior was destined to die by the shedding of blood. That way the Father could leave the flesh. After this separation, Jesus then commanded the spirit to leave (Lu. 23:46). Thus, the flesh of God suffered alone as the body of mortality took on immortality.

Throughout the scriptures the blood is emphasized to be important. It was sacrificed so the Father could leave His physical estate. Jesus had to give up His blood and with it His soul. This is what God promise to Eve (Gen. 3:15), that an Atonement would be made. Jesus became God in the flesh, to sacrifice His mortal body in order to atone for all men's sins. The Father emptied Himself from the flesh, the Spirit was commanded to leave, then the body was allowed to die. Three days later, His sinless body was retrieved. To show the immense power of godliness.

The divine events while Jesus stood on the cross is a constant reminder of immortality. God makes it an important point to emphasize the separation of the Deity when Jesus appears to Mary Magdalene and says: "Touch me not; for I am not yet ascended to my Father." (Jn. 20:17). After the resurrection, Jesus could be touched (Lu. 24:39).

Maintained by the spirit, Jesus stayed alive on the cross to suffer for our sins. His pain was almost unbearable as the Father could not look upon the horrible scene, prompting Jesus to cry out: "My God, my God, why hast thou forsaken me (Mk. 15:34).

No one but God could perform this way. You and I could not do this. When our souls leave us, we die. The Spirit stayed with Jesus until He commanded it to leave (Lu. 23:46). Thus Jesus subjected the flesh to suffer the *will* of the Father (Lu. 22:42), the Father breaking the bonds of death, giving the Son (flesh) power over the resurrection of the spiritual dead, and restoring them to their mortal bodies.

The "Comforter" Jesus talks about in John 14:16 is the Spirit (not soul) of God. "Nevertheless I tell you the truth; it is expedient for you that I go away: for if I do not go away the Comforter will not come unto you; but if I depart, I will send him unto you" (Jn.

16:7), "Even the Spirit of truth; whom the world cannot receive" (not while the spirit resided exclusively with Jesus) "because it seeth him not, neither knoweth him; for he dwelleth with you and shall be in you" (Jn. 14:17). *"For by one Spirit are we all baptized into one body,* whether we be Jews or Gentiles, whether we be bond or free; and have been all made to drink into the spirit" (I Cor. 12:13). Jesus is not here in the flesh but He can be near all of us and warm our hearts with guidance into the knowledge about His kingdom if we can just make the connection.

We must then realize that our brain houses our soul, and our soul belongs to God. "So also the soul of the son is mine" (Ez. 18:4) The human brain is millions of times more powerful in the subconscious than it is in the conscious.

Anciently, man lived knitted so well together that they could use their minds to levitate stones, to make pyramids and temples. This art has been lost through diversification and pragmatism. Occasionally one hears of five ton truck being lifted off a man's son in an accident, a miraculous healing, or a psychic who sees things. Such people have tapped the subconscious matrix, but they do not exercise a high degree of control over what they are doing. Just imagine what a gathering like Promise Keepers could do if their minds would melt together on one object? They could move the Empire State building (I Cor. 13:2).

Once you are able to develop spiritual thinking, minor miracles start happening in your life. They will continue to happen if you can keep Satan out of you subconscious. This is where his demons like to dwell. They like to make you all creatures of habit.

After the universe is melted by a "fervent heat," God's glory will illuminate the heavens. It is not known whether earth's plants and animals have a place in heaven. There are angels to be directed by redeemed beings (1 Cor. 6:3). It is said the redeemed will become part of the body of God. How wonderful it would be to have minds together. "For the body is not one member, but many. If the foot shall say, Because I am not the hand, I am not of the body; is it therefore not of the body" (I Cor. 12:14–15).

"And if Christ be in you, the body is dead because of sin; but the Spirit is life because of righteousness" (Rom. 8:10). "But if the Spirit of him that raised up Jesus from the dead dwell in you, he that raised up Christ from the dead shall also quicken your mortal bodies by the Spirit that dwelleth in you" (Rom 8:11). We alone determine whether our souls remain cut off (dead in spirit) or become alive in Christ. There is no way we can obligate God by our good works. It is our attitude that counts.

Jesus never concealed the fact that He was one in the same with the Father. Jesus would say many times that the Father was his driving source. He referred to the invisible Father residing within Him. Jesus speaks of the Father as "my Father" (Lu. 10:22; Mt. 11:27; 12:50; Jn. 20:17) or as "your Father" (Mt. 5:45, 48; Mark 11:25; Jn. 16:10), but Jesus *never* referred to God as "Our Father."

Check this out. Jesus does instruct you and me to use the term "Our Father" when we pray, but Jesus, being both the Father and the Son, would not use the expression to describe Himself. To do so would give the Father a separate distinguish outside His self. That separation did not happen until Jesus bled to death.

Disobedience put a change in Adam and Eve's body. They became mortal. Spiritually cut off from God. Now, Jesus has brought His kingdom on earth, a believing soul does not have to die. Such a soul may become absent from the body, but if it gains the spirit, it is forever present with Christ (I Cor. 5:3). When the body is called again from the grave, it will become spiritual in nature. Like the body of Jesus after His resurrection. One will be able to walk through walls, or upon water, like Peter did as he demonstrated the power of his subconscious mind while yet in the flesh.

The saved ones will take up bodies again to live on earth with Jesus during His millennial reign. That's when it "will be done on earth as it is in heaven." Until that time, our spirits acts within like a rubber band. One can stretch it thin, and a few actually lose it (1 Sam. 28:16).

Adam knew God and then fell. So did Saul (II Sam. 7:15). How about the once–glorious Satan? He had full faculties of what he was doing. There is no way that Satan may justify himself. When God is through with him, he will be lost forever.

It is God who quickens your soul to mesh with His spirit, but sometimes man will sin until they loses it. There are some with a limited knowledge of Jesus who fall into sin. Some are church officials with persuasive powers. Satan can take over your subconscious and make you feel depressed. The quickest way out of such a depression is to grab your Bible and read.

When God came to earth, he deprived himself of His own Holy Spirit. He fashioned Himself as a mortal babe. When the Spirit fell upon Jesus at His baptism, God had then successfully invaded, and functioned as divine, within the dominion of Satan.

Thus he "hath broken down the middle wall of partition between us" (Eph. 2:14), and re-established His heavenly kingdom on earth. God's Spirit now dwells all over the earth and only sin can keep it from each of us.

Jesus became God personified in the flesh when He received the manifestation of the spirit (Col. 2:9). Man on earth will never receive such a full manifestation of the Spirit because undoubtedly our eyes are not refined enough to see demons. So we remain imperfect, akin to earthly standards, that cloud and distort our spiritual thinking. Jesus tried to provoke spiritual thinking by using parables and open ended expressions. He found it difficult to keep His own apostles attuned to spiritual insight. Once a lesson is learned in spirit, it remains so long as the spirit dwells in you. Jesus returned His Spirit to "bring all things to your remembrance, whatsoever I have said unto you" (Jn. 14:26). How does one think God's words stayed with us those first hundred years? Before they were written down by Matthew, Mark, Luke, and John? God is not a man that He can lie (Titus 1:2). Remember the fig tree? The subsequent condemnation of the tree shows the way Jesus had command over the elements (See Mt. 9:6). Consider the love of God, as He allowed Himself to be spat upon and afflicted by other men? And render Him such an atrocious death. All the time those cold-hearted men whipped and tried Him "He open not his mouth" (Isa. 53:7). Should Jesus have opened His mouth in distress, His words would have condemned all of his pursuers eternally. They would all have dropped dead until they stacked up like cord wood. Sure God could have saved himself, but by enduring Satan's action against Him, Jesus opted to save the world. Why? Because "they know no not what they do" (Lu. 23:34)

Just as the soul gives life to your body, the Father gave life to the body of Jesus. "…if you had known me, ye should have known

my Father also" (Jn. 8:19). "I live by the Father (Jn. 6:57). "The
Father is in me" (Jn. 14:10). "Believe me that I am in the Father,
and the Father is in me: or else believe me for the very works sake"
(Jn. 14:11).

Seven times in the Bible Jesus refers to Himself as the "I Am."
The Jewish people knew exactly what Jesus was saying, and they
resented Him for speaking with such authority. His own community tried to kill Him when He first made such a pronouncement
(Lu. 4:17–29). As Jesus continued to preach with authority the
ruling authorities turned against Him (Mt. 9:2; Mark 2:5; Lu.
5:20, 23; 7:47). They came to understand Jesus was comparing
His personal life to their symbols that were embodied in their
scared temple at Jerusalem.

Jesus was not referring to his own flesh and bone body when
he said: "Verily, verily, I say unto you, before Abraham was, I am"
(Jn. 8:58). He was referring to source. His oun soul, or the Father's,
who was dwelling from within (Jn. 14:10).

We must always remember that God is capable of doing *anything* (Mt. 19:26; Mark 10:27; Lu. 18:27). Rocks and the wind
are subject to his command (See Lu. 19:40; Mt. 8:26). If God is
all powerful, why does He allow wars, individual sufferings and
personal strife (Born deformed etc.)? Again, God does not inter-
fere with man, and such causes might be traced back for generations (Ex. 20:5). But God does assure us that He saves the innocent.

Had Israel followed God's instructions, pollution might not
have corrupted at least one nation. Today we understand how dis-

eases are passed from one generation to the next. Let us learn from the past, and be satisfied for today, that the power of God does resides on earth today to make these things right for the future. Those mentally incapacitated are innocent, and as such, they may become a blessing to others.

All of us who traverse this earth should look beyond our short lives for answers to hard questions. This earth is our place of discovery. Take Daniel 10, Revelation 12, the Book of Jude, and lay them to the side of Paul's informative words: "For we wrestle not against flesh and blood, but against principalities, against powers, against the rulers of darkness in high places" (Eph. 6:12). Though God can zap Satan anytime He wants, He uses him to refine and shape men. God shows all due respect to the agency of men as He permits men to learn from the consequence of their own actions. Man had perfection with God in an Eden paradise, then blew it. Paradise has once again been made available to man by Jesus, if we but avail ourselves to it (Lu. 23:43).

Love cannot be forced, especially by the ones who are receiving it. True love for God should include a respect for those who oppose us. Learning about our satanic adversities allows us to appreciate spiritual good. The Lord chasteneth those he loves the most (Rev. 3:19; Heb. 12:6). If you can endure some chastening, praise God for it, for it may come to make you grow and be active. "God dealeth with you as sons; for what son is he who the father chasteneth not" (Heb. 6, 7).

The Jewish people rejected Jesus as their true Messiah because they followed the thoughts of their forefathers. Jesus tried to get men to think by speaking in parables. Jesus announced who He was and the parameters of His earthly ministry when He stopped

reading from Isaiah 61. He "closed the book" in the middle of
verse 2, where it says: "and the day of vengeance of our God." Jesus
was not here in the flesh to bring vengeance. That comes at judgment day.

    The Jewish people erred in their expectancy about the Messiah.
They were led to expect someone to throw off the yoke of their
Roman oppressors. Had they understood their Messiah's twofold
mission, they would have looked for a "servant" as described in
Isaiah 42. The Jews were counting down the seventy year promise
by Daniel. To them it was the end of their 69th year week. They
expected their Messiah (Dan. 9:24–27). They did not understand
there way to glory was going to be stopped by another gap in time
by adding a period of grace. During the time the Messiah would
be "cut off" to them. True, Daniel had promised the Jews their
Messiah would "restore and to build Jerusalem unto the Messiah"
(Dan. 9:25). The Jews should have realized their Messiah could
not perform this because their temple already stood. This is why
Jesus closed the book and stopped reading before He came to the
physical aspects of the prophesy (Dan. 9:26; Lu. 4:18; Isa. 61:2).
The Jewish thinking at the time demanded a Messiah who would
bring vengeance upon the Romans.

    Jesus will return after the grace period is over for the Gentiles.
If we know the scriptures, we will understand that Jesus has a duel
purpose to preform when He comes again. He will first rebuild
the Jewish temple as prophesied (Zech. 6:12–13; Dan. 9:25).
This erection of the Jewish temple in Jerusalem will activate
Daniel's seventh-year countdown for the Jewish people again. Their
final seven years shall be known as the times of "tribulations" (Mt.
24:21). The temple will be built during a brief time of chaos in
the world that shocks the world Jew in returning to Israel.
    Most Christian Churches have nothing to say about these end

time events. Few mention that Jesus is supposed to build and restore the Jewish temple in Jerusalem. It seem by now christianity
is over looking Bible prophesy about Jesus return to restore the
Jewish temple. Its reconstruction means little to a christian, but it
does have a significant meaning to the Jews: "Behold the man
whose name is The *Branch*; and he shall grow up out of his place,
and he shall build the temple of the Lord" (Zech. 6:12).

When the "end times" of the Gentiles is "fulfilled" (Lu. 21:24),
God will renew the seventy year covenant with the Jews just where
He stopped it in its 69th year. At that time chaos will subside as
politics in the world revert back to the way it was when Jesus was
alive.

What confuses todays theologians about this time is the unusual activity of Jesus. He is to return to the Jewish people first,
and the rest of the world will not see Him. They just hear rumors
because communications will be down at the time. Out of chaos
will come ten world ruling kings, to be followed by the anti-christ,
who succeeds to devour these ten kings and establish a world ruling empire. Jesus will smash this empire and then establish a paradise on earth that will last for a thousand years.

During this thousand years of righteous reign, Jesus will be
our king, and things will be done on earth as they are done in
heaven. Satan will be bound for this thousand year period, then he
will be Loosened for a while to tempt those who grew up during
those thousand years without any temptation. Next comes eternity, where the righteous will dwell with God and the unrigh-
teous will be judged to dwell with Satan. Forever!

ISRAEL

Revelations chapter 12 draws us a "thumbnail" sketch that covers the plight of Israel down through biblical history. Inserted in that same chapter is a flashback to explain the disposition of Satan. This chapter shows the long struggle Israel has with the devil.

Those who overcome by "the blood of the Lamb" (V. 11) include the lost children of Israel. The woman in verse 14 depicts all Israel, but notice there are two of them in the last days. One returns under God's grace, (The Gentiles) and the other (The Jews) will continue to suffer until they must flee into the wilderness 3½ years before Armageddon. Revelation 12 can be confusing unless one considers the dualistic nature of the prophesy. How two places can be called "Israel," at the same time.

God is not a man that he should lie (See Isa. 46:10). When God makes a vow, it will be done (Isa. 55:11). Read God's promises to Abraham, Isaac, and Jacob. Then review the blessings of Jacob upon his grandsons Ephraim and Manasseh (Gen. Ch. 48). Next, review the blessings bestowed upon Jacob's own twelve sons (Genesis Ch 49). Note how the descendants of Abraham shall grow in the world until they become a great influence over all other nations (See Gen. 22:17,18).

The Bible is a record of how the promises made to all Israel would turn out down through history. There would be some telling, and very unusual event to take place among God's chosen people. How they were cultured in Egypt, refined in the Siani, and scattered from the nation of Israel. How the scattering of Israel could bring about God's great promise that all of the world would be blessed is now starting to focus. But first we must learn to distinguish what the Bible prophesies pertain to the lost ten tribes of Israel, and what prophesy pertains to the Jews.

The prophet Isaiah put a label on God's mysterious work during grace. He said it would be "a marvelous work and a wonder" (Isa. 29:14). One does not hear many sermons delivered upon this subject. Perhaps because it is not generally known or understood, that this prophesy takes place under grace, and that grace has been extended to the lost ten tribes of Israel. Those hidden among the Gentiles for the last two thousand years. A time when knowledge is to be increased (Hab. 2:14). If men fail to understand this, it will be because their natural eyes remain fastened upon worldly knowledge and human expectations. Under the weight of human emotions the Bible can be misconstrued.

A similar lust for power became the stumbling blocks for the Jews. They allowed their priests to lead the whole nation into error when they concocted the Book of Deuteronomy. From it they made up the new law of Moses (TORAH). At this instant, God withdrew from them and described destruction upon them through the prophet Jeremiah. From 587 BC onward, the Jews would become a satalite nation to four world ruling empires. After 70 AD the Jews would also be scattered throughout the world.

The Jewish people erred back in 612 BC, when they decided all biblical prophecy applied to just them. They did not consider that the Bible might pertain to another. They established their

Torah law to strict that it now excluded their brethren lost in the north. They saw only their demise as they mixed their blood with their captors. We shall see how the Jews erred in this assessment.

The ancient religious style of the Jews was seriously altered during the reformations of a boy king about 600 B.C. During the reign of King Josiah the priests claimed they had found another book in their temple that had been written by Moses. This*deuto*, or second book of Moses, is recorded in the Bible today as "Deuteronomy." Being found in about 612 B.C. would mean the book had laid dormant during some of Israel's more famous history.

It is hard to conceive how such an important item would go unnoticed during the conquests of Zion, their rise to a world dominating power, their temple building era, and through the dividing of kingdoms, the prophet Isaiah's time, and thus remain hidden through the religious reformations of King Hezekiah one hundred and thirty four years earlier. Not to mention how this important book was not used by two of Israels greatest judges, Samuel and Elijah. It is important to put this book into its perspective, because its so called discovery is responsible for current Jewish religious thought.

Deuteronomy has become the focus point in current Israeli law. It underscore the other four books of Moses, as it forms the Jewish *Torah*. This new religious mode started among the Jews during young king Josiah's reformations about 600 B.C. What the Torah does is establish the Jewish priests in positions of supremacy over the law. The priests used this newly found book elevate them in stature to positions of power. A power that had eluded them since they were subjected to the prophets and their Kings. This is not a altogether a new attempt for the priests. They tried to usurp

Moses religious authority back in the days of Mt. Siani (See Num.
16:32).

The Torah placed the prophet and the King under the religious
control of the law that was now being interpreted by the priests.
This was done against the will of a prophetess (II Kings 22:10–
16; II Chron. 34:22–24), Of course they did not dare involve
Jeremiah who was alive at the time.

God did love king Josiah, but He disapproved of what the
priests were doing under his reign. God rejected Josiah's reformation by name (Jer. 3:6). Jeremiah now warned the Jewish people of
their impending destruction. The Jews refused to believe Jeremiah
because of their status as a blessed nation. Just thirteen year later
they would see Jeremiah's prophesies come true.

When King Josiah died, Israel was attacked and defeated by
the Babylonians. After fifty years of captivity the Jews were allowed to return to Jerusalem. Ezra, a priest, took charge of this
exodus, but he reinstated the *Torah*! He used its dictatorial powers
to control those from among them who returned to Jerusalem.

The synagogues became an extension of the priests power to
use them to extend their power and indoctrinate the Jewish people.
Thus it remains for all descendants right down to our present day.
Jesus ministered contrary to the Torah's ridged laws. Often they
tried to use the law to destroy Jesus.

Jeremiah saw there new religion established (Jer.31:33). Jesus
did not put new wine into old bottles (Mr. 2:22). Rather, what Jesus
did was to put all of the Mosaic law into a shadow as he made a new
law a reality.

Thus Josiah's religious system survived after Israel's defeat by the Babylonians in 587 B.C. It remained in place while Jesus walked the earth. It still maintains a social religious control over the Jewish communities today. When Jesus suggested something quite different and profound in his own synagogue, the Jewish people rose up against him with dyer rejection, and attempted to kill him then (Lu. 4:18–29).

Down through the many torturous years the Jews have maintained their autonomy in the world perhaps because of their deep rigid religious traits. Their perilous plight over the past two thousand years can be traced to their strong family units as their laws suggests.

Back in 600 B.C. Hilkiah the priest approached Huldah the prophetess for her blessing upon the new book they found in the temple. Her evaluation was: "Thus saith the Lord, Behold, I will bring evil upon this place, and upon the inhabitants thereof, even all the curses that are written in the book which they have read before the king of Judah" (II Chron. 34:24). The prophet Jeremiah virtually accused the priests of writing the book themselves (Jer. 8:8), and by doing this evil deed, they had turned God's house into "a den of robbers" (Jer. 7:4–11).

In spite of the prophetic warnings, the priests were able to gain the favor of the young king and used the new book as part of his reformation. The harsh laws imposed by the priests finds a place into christianity as they use its restrictive nature to develop church by-laws.

Now that we have arrived at the last days, a time when God has told us we can gain new understanding (Heb. 2:14), our world becomes stifled by other restrictive religious standards. New ideas are discouraged in spite of the fact that 'God will pour out his spirit on all flesh (Joel 2:28). We now have the Bible published to all the world in fulfillment of prophecy (Mr. 13:10). What we need to do now is take a fresh look at it.

The northern ten tribes of Israel may be lost in the world so far as men can see, but they have never been lost from the view of God (Ez. 34:11–13). In the last days lost Israel and the Jewish nation will be brought together (Ez. 37:21–24). God is very poetic when he talks about lost Israel in the Bible. God wants them to remain lost in the world until this end-time-era. (This time of grace)

To understand God's poetic message about all Israel, we must review some important blessings bestowed upon the heads of Ephraim and Manasseh by their grandfather Jacob. Manasseh was to become a single great nation, and Ephraim was to become a multitude of nations (Gen. 48:19). When Israel split into two separate nations, Jeroboam, an Ephraimite, became king over the northern ten tribes (1 Kings 11:31). The descendants of Ephriam and Manasseh became part of the northern kingdom. After this respect, the northern kingdom was called "Israel" (1 Kings 12:20). Solomon's son Rehoboam continued upon the throne of David, but all that remained of his kingdom were the territories of Judah and Benjamin (1 Kings 12:21).

Name distinction is very important to follow the scriptures directed toward lost Israel. Rehoboam's small kingdom in Jerusalem is often referred to as of Judah (I Kings 12:27). The term "Jew" is first used in scripture to describe when the southern kingdom of Judah marched upon the northern "king of Israel" (II Kings

16:6–7). The Jews may be called Israel too, but they are only a part of all Israel. When a prophet uses the term "all Israel," both the lost ten tribes and the Jews are included. When just the term "Israel" is used, it usually means that portion of Israel that became lost.

The Jewish people are the only part of Israel who has remained largely identifiable. It takes spiritual guidance and Bible knowledge to identify lost Israel in the world. There are some scriptures that are directed only to them (See II Sam. 7:10). In some areas on this earth their blood may be more concentrated.

To identify where lost Israel is more heavily concentrated for the last days is to consider those nations who seem to be blessed (Mt. 7:20). According to Samuel, one of these nations will be exceedingly blessed. So much so that they will in turn bless all other nations. An accurate description of the United States of America.

The Jews may had slid out of favor with God for the last 2600 years, but they are still a blessed people. God cares for them, but under grace, God works directed more toward those of Israel who were anciently lost. Their "offspring" are being used to fulfill God's blessings to Abraham: "All the families of the earth shall be blessed (Gen. 12:3).

Jesus directed that His true gospel be sent to the Gentiles (Acts 13:47). This "good news" has been bringing souls to Jesus for the last two thousand years. The New Testament refers to this activity as the separation of the wheat from the tares (Mt. 13:38). The good fruit seems to be coming from among the Gentiles throughout the world.

Christianity recognizes salvation through grace, but when Christianity was adopted by the Roman state, it became deluded in spirit when it became controlled by man. Men who decided all religious knowledge was complete. Then they categorized the subjectivist who thought "learn" means to accept on faith. Religion became a code of ethics. Those who would not go along with church prescribed ethics were considered heretics. An independent approach to God that did not go along with the code could cost you your life..

Theories, ideas, and discoveries are not revealed to men collectively under grace. They have been the products of men. The pressure of MENS IDEAS brought about the renaissance, the discovery of new worlds and new ideas. This protest era is now called "the age of reason."

Lets review one very important promise made to all Israel as found in II Samuel 7:10. "Moreover I will appoint a place for my people Israel, and I will plant them, that they may dwell in a place of their own, and move no more; neither shall the children of wickedness afflict them any more, as before time." According to this prophecy we should look for the descendants of *lost Israel to swell up* in some nation which is fertile and has abundance.

We find more information on this subject in Ezekiel 34:14. "I will feed them in a good pasture, and upon the high mountains of Israel." High mountains would place them above many nations. Isaiah says they will be "established in the top of the mountains, and be exalted above the hills, and all nations shall flow unto it" (Isa. 2:2). This is a very accurate description of the United States of America!

These verses do not describe the nation of Israel in Jerusalem today. It will never apply to them, because they encourage only the Jewish people to flow into their nation; yet scholars and ministers try to attribute these scriptures to the country of Israel we know today. This is because no one since early Christianity has bothered to consider the plight of lost Israel in the Bible.

Consider this special nation that some will be planted in. It will be a place of their own, they shall not be moved, and they shall never be *afflicted*. One things for sure, this can not apply to the Jews in Palestine. They have been afflicted since day one. This has to be a nation like the U.S.A. We may have problems from the inside, but if we are that blessed nation, we will never be conquered. We shall see later that the U.S.A. will indeed be attached by outside forces, and how God will repel that attack with natural forces.

Is the United States now fulfilling Bible prophesy? Some will not see it that way, but who has truly remained unafflicted since the old Roman Empire? Who else but north and South America? Of course these continents never did come under Roman rule.

In Isaiah Ch. 42 we have the Messiah's mission on earth outlined as a servant, but he also make a covenant with the Gentiles (Isa. 42:6). "Behold, I shall do a new thing.." (Isa. 43:18–19), and in Isaiah Ch. 44 the "new thing" is explained if one includes the first five verses of Ch. 45.

Isaiah addresses both lost Israel and the Jews as chapter 44 opens. Isaiah assures the lost ten tribes they would "not be forgotten of me" (Vs. 21) if they return unto God, they would be "redeemed" (Vs. 22). How are they to be *redeemed*? "Fear not: for I am with thee: I will bring my seed from the east, and gather thee from the west" (Isa. 42: 5). Under God's grace, lost Israel has been called by His spirit, and we are being separated from the tares for the last two thousand years.

This is the marvelous work God describes way back in Isaiah Ch. 29. God explains a "marvelous work and wonder" would be preformed for lost Israel (Vs.14). Since the resurrection, God has been calling His "other sheep" (Jn. 10:16). He is seeking out His own according to the covenant found in Isaiah chapter 42. The Christian Churches should be elaborating upon this subject. One is not automatically saved when the spirit falls upon them during grace. What the believer feels is the "Spirit of adoption" (Rom. 8:15). From that moment on, God will work to develop you as His sons.

Jeremiah set about to lay the groundwork for this new covenant, by lifting up the Zarah line. Zarah was one of Judah's twins who also received a special birthright promise (Gen. 38:27–30). It fell upon Jeremiah to heal this breach. Some biblical scholars, who have tried to make some sense out of the 38th chapter of Genesis, trace the Zarah line to the throne in the British Isles. This, they explain, is how another biblical prophesy is fulfilled: "And thine house and thy kingdom shall be established forever before thee: thy throne shall be established forever" (II Sam. 7:16; I Chron. 17:12; II Chron. 7:18).

We know from the Bible that God removed Judah and her kings (II kings 23:27). This happened after Josiah's reformation as Deuteronomy only allows the king to function at the behest of the priests. When the priest Ezra restored the Jewish people to Jerusalem after fifty years of captivity, there was no longer a strong king.

We see the extent of this kingly matter when king Herod of Jesus day was of mixed blood.

Things did not go well for Israel after the kingdoms split. The northern kingdom ways became so bad the built bull-calves to mark it borders. They took themselves out of the influence of the ARK of the Covenant. This ark gave them symbols to guide them and their faith.

It is easy to trace Israel in the Bible. A king got in the way. King Manasseh made Judah and the inhabitants of Jerusalem err. He did worse than the heathen whom the Lord had destroyed before (II Chron. 33:9). He did evil in the sight of the Lord by placing graven images and altars in the temple. At this point in time, about 800 B.C., it is said by some scholars that the ark of the covenant was taken from the temple because God would not allow His religious symbol to occupy the same area with pagan religious symbols.

There is no mention of the holy ark being among the precious inventory taken from Jerusalem when the Babylonians defeated Judah in 587 B.C Either it was hidden or taken from the city before that time. Some scholars think it is Ethiopia and is being used by an unusual Christian sect there, but that is a subject for another book.

A brief history leading to Josiah's reformations finds King Manasseh's son Amon reigned two years and transgressed. His servants slew him in his own house. Then others rose up and killed the servants who killed Amon (II Chron. 33:21–25). These events along with others illustrate the evil present in Israel just prior to young king Josiah. Bear in mind that He came to power when he was eight years old.

One can see the desire for the priest Hilkiah to assert some kind of authority in Israel. His call for a reformation was popular even though it would take the kings of Judah out of primary religious authority. Thereafter the prophets were relegated to wear sackcloth and had no authority over the priests.

Many of the ancient prophets were given a glimpse into the future as they prophesied for both the visible and lost Israels. Without the historical knowledge we have today it would be very hard for the early Christian churches to have understood some of the prophecies pertaining to our last days. We come out of the reformations of our own sixteenth century with little regard to future prophecy, but now we have an increase of knowledge. This writing is a review of that latter-day prophecy.

It has taken years to receive the "good news" of the gospel throughout the spiritual hearts concentrated among the descendants of lost Israel in this world. If the United States is indeed that protected place set aside for the descendants of lost Israel, we are very recent to biblical history, but words that identify the United States do come alive in the Bible. One does not need to speculate or rely on faith alone. It is all there in Bible if we just get rid of that one book that distorts it. Throw away the Book of Deuteronomy. Go around such stumbling blocks. Use the wisdom to know spiritual things (See Mt. 24:43; Rev. 13:18).

The unafflicted nation spoken of in II Samuel 7:10 would have to be a nation with a strong concentration of Israelite blood.

We know the lost tribes of Israel were driven northward. From there we can assume they sifted throughout Europe and on to England, from England and the rest of Europe to the United States. Then the United States becomes such a bastion of freedom others are drawn to it (Isa. 2:2).

Some minor prophetic signs are now becoming apparent. Earthquakes, wars, pestilence, erratic weather, and decreasing human morals are some signs for us to watch for in the last days. "Behold, the days come, saith the Lord God, that I will send a famine in the land, not a famine of bread, nor a thirst for water, but of hearing the words of the Lord. And they shall wander from sea to sea and from the north, even to the east, they shall run to and fro to seek the word of the Lord, and shall not find it" (Amos 8:11–12). Not unless they find it in God's book, and to those who do: "he will shew you things to come" (Jn. 16:13).

Prophecy reveals itself clearly to those who trace it with two Israels in mind. The Jews are those whom we can know, and the others are the "lost sheep" Jesus spoke about. Under grace, the lost ones of Israel, are surfacing for truth all around the world.

One prophet who speaks to the Jews only is Daniel. He establishes a framework that incorporates all of biblical prophesy. So extensive were his prophecies that Daniel did not understand them himself. He asked God for the interpretation, and was told the prophesy was sealed: "Go thy way Daniel: for the words are closed up and sealed till the time of the end" (Dan. 11:8,9). He does not mention a word about God's marvelous works under grace.

Our vast communication systems of our modern world make the obscure words of Daniel come alive with new meanings. We no longer have to guess about prophecy. Latter day prophecy now unfolds in our daily newscasts.

Daniel is the first to introduce the term "messiah" (Dan. 9:25–26). A "messiah" becomes the central figure for both Jewish and Christian expectations. The Jews would not accept Jesus as their messiah because they were missled by their own priests. They had predetermined a role for their messiah. They looked for a messiah who would rid them of their enemies. They still do, but God does not to fill that promise for to them until he redeems the lost of Israel, now responding to Jesus under grace.

Instead of reestablishing the small Jewish nation to its once-glorious empire status, Jesus came to gather those who were lost (Lu. 19:20). Who was lost at the time? Not the Jews making up the tribes of Judah and Benjamin, but the other ten tribes of Israel.

The Jews did not become lost and scattered until 71 A. D. This eliminates the Jews from being the nation spoken of in II Sam. 7:10. The Palestine area does not at all fit the description of God's "appointed place" where Israel "will move no more." Where is this place? As previously suggested, it has to be the United States!

Jesus did come at Daniel's appointed time, (at the end of their sixtyninth year) leaving one year week left before the Jews come in to their glory (See Dan. 9:24). The Messiah will in that day return to build their temple when Daniel's count down for the resumes. At that time politics will return to the way they were before grace began.

The prophecy in Daniel 9:27 was delayed for the Jewish people when they rejected Jesus. Delayed until the gospel is preached unto the Gentile nations of this world (Mr. 13:10). When grace for the world is over, capitalism is going to fail an cause a change of politics. During this time the United States is going to be threatened by an outside invasion. Staying true to his word, God will repeal that coming invasion by natural causes (earthquakes, storms, etc). God saves this nation, and during those times, He Raptures His redeemed from off this earth to meet Him in the clouds. This means the redeemed will have a safe haven while the Jews and the rest of the world will go through a seven-year period called "tribulations."

The Jews used the term "Gentile" to describe all other people in ancient times (Gal. 3:14). This does not mean God is through with the Jewish people. Gentile is not the term Jesus uses to identify His lost in the world. The nation in Jerusalem at the last days will suffer threats until the final battle called "Armageddon" is waged there.

The Jewish nation of Israel is yet to gather all of this world's Jews. This will happen when all western nations go into chaos. Out of this chaos will come a strong political system that will resemble the old Roman Empire. This according to prophesies found in Daniel Ch. 2 and 7.

"For I would not, brethren, that ye should be ignorant of this mystery, lest ye should be wise in your own conceits; that blindness in part is happened to Israel, until the fullness of the Gentiles be come in" (Rom. 11:25). Grace is provided for all men, both the Jew and the Gentile. When the Jews rejected Jesus, He directed the gospel be sent among his lost sheep in the rest of the world (See Rom. 11:13; Jn. 10:27).

The covenant year week that God has remaining with the Jewish people is found in Daniel 9:27, but for almost two thousand years now it has been put on hold. Daniel's seventieth week begins again for the Jews when God is finished with his work to the Gentiles and recalls his spirit back to heaven (See II Thes. 2:7).

Jesus did not eliminate the seven remaining years allotted to the Jews (Dan. 9:24). He just postponed them. "For the vision is yet for an appointed time, but at the end it shall speak, and not lie: though it tarry, wait for it; because it will surely come, it will not tarry (Hab. 2:3). Wait for what? Wait for the "abomination of desolation, spoken of by Daniel the prophet" (Mt. 24:15).

The "abominations" to look for will be the rise of ten kings who will rule at the last days (See Dan. 2:41). During their reign the "man of sin," seen by both Daniel and Paul, is going to come into this world and rule it (See 2 Thes. 2:3; Dan. 2, 7).

Hosea is a prophet in northern Israel at the time the ten tribes were destroyed and otherwise deported by the Assyrians in 721 B.C. He is their prophet of doom, just as Jeremiah became southern Israel's prophet of doom one hundred thirty-four years later. He is the first to assure lost Israel that God will "ransom them from the power of the grave" (Hos. 1:14).

Hosea indicated the northern ten tribes would become lost in the world, that they "shall abide many days without a king, and without a sacrifice, and without an image, and without an ephod and without teraphim (Hos. 3:4). Then Hosea promised how their children would "return" to God in the "latter days" (Hos. 3:9).

This "marvelous work" (Isa. 29:14) has been happening among the Gentile nations from Jesus until now.

Isaiah was a prophet who lived in the southern Kingdom of Israel when the northern ten tribes were defeated. Isaiah's prophecies become far more involved than others. He covers both immediate and long-range incidents for both lost and visible Israel. Isaiah's prophecies speak to one segment of Israel and then to the other, which in turn causes our modern scholars to think there is more than just one prophet who writes under Isaiah's name. What scholars and theologians should consider, is the possibility of two separate Israel's, instead of two different Isaiahs. Isaiah is the first prophet to see all the way through to the future. He is the first to describe conditions on earth during Christ's millennial reign (See Isa. 11:5–10).

Almost one-half of Isaiah's prophecies pertain to the lost children of Israel. The other half pertain to the Jewish nation. Isaiah was very detailed in his prophecy concerning the return of the Jews to Jerusalem under King Cyrus of Persia in 537 B.C.

Isaiah used modifying terms to locate lost Israel. Notice how he uses words like "top of the mountain," "exalted," "an ensign," and often he uses the name "Israel."

Remember, the name "Israel" was bestowed by Jacob upon Ephraim and Manassah (Gen. 48:16). These are they "whose branches run over the wall" (Gen. 49:22). Again, what wall, and where are they?

Isaiah was the first to predict the coming Immanuel (Isa. 7:14). He describes the manner in which he should die (Isa. 52:13–15). He was accurate about this, and toward the end Isaiah sees a great heat flash on the earth as the redeemed rapture into the clouds to meet the returning Jesus (Isa. 30:26).

God told Isaiah that lost Israel's offspring would be "returned" unto God at the "last days" (Isa. 44:22). Jesus makes this possible through his atoning sacrifice. Now that God's spirit hovers over the earth, Jesus knows that: "My sheep hear my voice (Jn. 10:27).

Jesus has been calling home His lost sheep for the last two thousand years. "For I will pour water upon him that is thirsty, and floods upon thy seed, and my blessing upon thine offspring: and they shall spring up as among the grass (wheat among the tares) (Mt. 13:29) as willows by the water courses. *One shall say, I am the LORD's; and another shall subscribe with his hand unto the LORD, and surname himself by the name of Israel*" (Isa. 44:3–5, underlining added) "After those days" (after the sacrifice is complete) "saith the LORD, I will put my law in their inward parts, and write it in their hearts; and I will be their God, and they shall be my people" (Jer.31:33).

The Jews still do not understand this scripture, because it states the case for spiritual redemption. The Jews still believe in sacrifice, yet God spoke with Jeremiah and predicted their religious ways would be altered. It is Jesus who writes the spiritual law into men's hearts by bringing to this earth His new spiritual kingdom. Jesus becomes the sacrifice, and his atonement gave *all* who believe a chance to be saved (Ps. 102:15–18).

By extending his love through grace, God fulfills all that was promised upon the seed of Abraham. Through Abraham's seed, all the nations on earth will be blessed (Gen. 18:18; Gal. 3:8). For thousands of years now, Abraham's genetic code has dispersed itself by the mixing of blood. Some alive today may have a higher concentration of Israelite blood than others.

By dispersing lost Israel God has provided a way to do His marvelous work right under Satan's nose—but look out! If you respond to God's truth, Satan can easily spot you (See I Peter 5:8). Now you are in for a new set of problems. People who once loved you may turn on you. Jesus warned us about this (Mt. 10:24).

When the promise of a redeemer was made to Eve (Gen. 3:15), Satan may have thought he could usurp God by having Cain kill Abel. Satan knew exactly where to attack when all the promises of God were vested in one man, one family, or one nation. By dispersing Israel throughout all the nations, God made it difficult for Satan to identify exactly where God's chosen people really are.

We can also recognize our spiritual brethren as they respond to God's spiritual gift. In like manner, we can recognize them among this world of nations. We know where they are as they swell up within nations. The largest concentration of spiritual and forgiving children has swelled up in these the United States. We fit God's blessed nation the way we draw out of this world those who wish to be free also (See Jn. 8:32).

The Bible gives us other examples of how God's wisdom is greater than the cunning of the devil. God cast some confusion over whose line held the scepter promise. Read about this in the thirty eight chapter of Genesis. In his attempt to disrupt the scepter promise to Judah, Satan corrupted the first two sons of Judah, to the extent that *God killed them*. As the story goes, Tamar produced a very important set of twins in a strange encounter. They were sired from her own stepfather.

When Genesis 38 is carefully read, we find God is confusing Satan so that he does not know whether to follow Pharez or Zerah line. Look at the thirty seventh chapter of Ezekiel, where "He cropped of the top of his young twigs, and carried it into a land of traffick; he set it in a city of merchants." This does describe Britain in later years, but a separate book is needed to describe all involved in these puzzling verses. In Genesis chapter 38, God is playing games with the devil that leaves many confused.

The game involves hiding lost Israel in the world. Ezekiel explains that all Israel comes together in the millennium (Ez. 37:15–18). The coming together so noted here must sound confusing to those who try to read Ezekiel with only one segment of Israel in mind. Two separate segments of Israel must become established in your mind before we can study Ezekiel chapters 38 and 39 later.

During God's gift of grace, Satan scampers to and fro to hinder God"s work, while all this time more souls are recognizing the truth than at any other time in biblical history. While Satan's ministers are preaching half truths, they play right into God's hands as they strike spiritual chords within the hearts of God's blessed people. Yes, truth can be gleaned and evaluated, no matter where it comes from (Phil. 1:18).

Satan's ministers and his false-teaching churches will indeed become more successful toward the end. Prosperity will lead most people to rely on established norms instead of God's word. About the time truth seems to be snuffed out, God is going to wipe away everyone's prosperity (See Ez. 7). This throws the western world into chaos and ends our present period of grace.

The remaining small nation of Judah (southern two tribes) were themselves defeated by Babylon approximately one hundred thirty four years after the northern ten tribes were deported north and lost. It was during the occupation of Judah when God raised up the prophet Daniel to reassure the Jewish people. Daniel assured the Jews that God had a future in mind for them too. During Daniel's own lifetime the occupying Babylonians were defeated by the Persians, and their King Cyrus allowed the Jews to return to Jerusalem. This world be 537 B.C. Just fifty years after being captured by the Assyrians

Jewish autonomy was maintained during their return when the prophet Ezra closely scrutinized the genealogy of those returning to Jerusalem in 535 B.C. Mixed marriages had to be dissolved, and those who could not prove their genealogy were not allowed to return. The prophet Ezra was strict about screening the known genealogies until those Jews returning from exile were considered all that was left of the house of "Israel." Those who were unable to prove their identities were considered to be "Gentiles."

By the priest Ezra's actions during this exodus, the Jewish "Torah" was reconfirmed. Some say Ezra was perhaps the one who added a few words to Deuteronomy to give Moses a burial (Deut. 34:5–11). Moses could not have penned these words if he were already dead?

Perhaps it was Deuteronomy that caused the priests to discard some other books mentioned in the Bible. A Book of Jashar is referred to in Josh. 10:3 and again in II Sam. 1:18. The prophet Jehu is referred to in I Kings 16:12. There are books like Gad (I Chron. 29:29–30), and the prophesies of Ahiu (II Chron. 9:29). These books are not in the Bible today. Perhaps the priests used these lost books to help them make up Deuteronomy, then discard them so no one could prove their forgery. Yes, Jesus is known to quote words found in Deuteronomy, but they could have been words the priests pieced together from these lost sources.

"Then the Lord said unto me, the prophets prophesy lies in my name: I sent them not, neither have I commanded them, neither spake unto them: they prophesy unto you a false vision and divination, and a thing of nought, and the deceit of their heart. Therefore thus saith the Lord concerning the prophets that prophesy in my name, and I sent them not, yet they say, sword and famine shall not be in this land; By sword and famine shall those prophets be consumed" (See Jer. 14:14–15)

Thirteen years after this prophecy by Jeremiah, all Israel was "consumed." If Daniel could not understand the writings of Jeremiah (Dan. 9:2–4), we can forgive the priest Ezra for he may be a victim of circumstances.

God's marvelous work during grace has done much to fill some of the greater blessings He made to Abraham: "that Abraham shall become a great and mighty nation, and all nations of the earth shall be blessed in him" (Gen. 18:18). Israel did become an empire, but not all other nations were blessed at that time. All nations are not being blessed by the nation of Israel in our day, nor will they be, because God's promise to Abraham does not happen through the known nation of Israel today. God's spiritual kingdom is blessing the world today through those who can hear His voice (J. 10:27). On the other hand, all nations are being blessed right now through the *appointed* nation we know as the Untied States of America. People could not have know the full extent of God's promises to Abraham years ago because the United States did not exist.

Paul reminds us there are two parts involved in Abraham's promise (Gal. 4:24). The first promise to Abraham was that his offspring would become a "great and mighty nation" (Gen. 17:20). This occurred when Israel became an empire nation under kings David and Solomon.

The second part of Abraham's blessing is that through his seed "all the nations of the world would be blessed" (Gen.18:18). Undoubtably from a special nation appointed by God, a thriving nation because it will move no more, or ever be defeated.

We are living in a time when Abraham's second blessing is happening. First England, and then the United States, have become this world's greatest prognosticators of peace. England and the United States have buttressed the world from an evil takeover by Germany and Russia. England has done much to culture our modern day world. The United States is first in the advancement of new ideas and now finds us in a world leadership position. We are the melting pot of all cultures.

This is definitely in fulfillment of what Jacob promised to his son Joseph in Genesis 49:

"Joseph is a fruitful bough, even a fruitful bough by the well; whose branches run over the wall: The archers have sorely grieved him, and shot at him, and hated him. But his bow abode in strength, and the arms of his hands were made strong by the hands of the mighty God of Jacob; (from thence is the shepherd, the stone of Israel:) Even by the God of thy father, who shall help thee; and by the Almighty, who shall bless thee with blessings of heaven above, blessings of the deep that lieth under, blessings of the breasts, and of the womb: The blessings of thy father have prevailed above the blessings of my progenitors unto the utmost bound of the everlasting hills: they shall be on the head of Joseph, and on the crown of the head of him that was separate from his brethren" (Gen. 49:22–26).

Jacob had previously blessed the two sons of Joseph with his namesake (See Gen. 48:13–16). Jacob's namesake was Israel. God changed his name to Israel when he blessed him at Bethel (Gen. 35:10). This is important to know, because ancient prophets often refer to the lost ten tribes by calling them Israel. The Jews they call Judah (See I Kings 12:27), and then there are other references like "sons of Jacob," "Jerusalem," "Zion," and "Ephriamites".

Since the ancient prophets did not know how to describe grace, they used terms like "mighty people," or an "ensign" to the world! Our charitable attitude and contributions do not go unnoticed in the Bible. We are described as the "Mountain of the Lord's house" in Isaiah 2:2, where "all nations shall flow into it."

If the end is indeed close, then the United States has an important role. One can identify the United States in prophecy if he will conceive the fact that there are two separate Israels being addressed in Bible prophecy. We are challenged in the Bible to seek out such things (Matt. 24:44). See for yourself if we in the U.S. are the "mighty people," the "mountain of the Lord's house," and God's "ensign" to the world in this the last days. If you start to make those connections, it is done through understanding the more obscure vows and promises God made to Israel through the prophets.

Other than the personal salvation found in the New Testament, the Jewish people do not participate in God's holy blessings until the grace period is over. Jesus will appear to them to get them started the first part of tribulations (Zech. 12:10), and seven years later they will be welcomed to glory as all Israel meets together to preside over God's millennial reign.

TWO-PART COVENANT

Paul understood there was more than just one segment of Israel when he said: "And the scripture, foreseeing that God would justify the heathen through faith, preached before the gospel unto Abraham saying, In thee shall all the nations be blessed" (Gal. 3:8), "That the blessing of Abraham might come on the Gentiles through Jesus Christ; that we might receive the promise of the Spirit through faith" (Gal. 3:14).

The first covenant God made with Israel has already transpired. It was consummated at Mount Sinai (Gal.4:24; Ex. 19:6–8), and completed when Israel became a great empire some 2,950 years ago. The second part of God's two-part covenant was not put into effect until the advent of Jesus Christ. This second covenant was put in force after His sacrifice and subsequent resurrection.

"Therefore, behold, I will proceed to do a marvelous work among this people, even a marvelous work and wonder: for the wisdom of the wise men shall perish, and the understanding of their prudent men shall be hid" (Isa. 29:14). "In thy seed shall all the nations of the earth be blessed." This second blessing transpires under God's marvelous work (Gen. 26:4; Gal. 3:7–8, 4:24). It is being done through "*prudent men*" who "*shall be hid.*"

Abraham was blessed that his children will multiply until they become as numerous as the "stars of heaven, and as the sand which is upon the seashore" (Gen. 22:17).

There are approximately thirty million Jews in the world today. In order for their numbers to be like the stars, we will have to number the *hidden ones*. This figure would have to be huge. To ponder the number makes us aware of just how deluded the blood of lost Israel is and the vast way that it has been mixed through out the world. History would tell us that only a small portion is mixed with China, India, and the African aborigines. Most has been hidden then in the western nations of the world.

"Look unto me, and be ye saved, all the ends of the earth: for I am God, and there is none else" (Isa. 45:22). Isaiah saw that God would come to earth, be smitten, and die for the sins of men (Isa. 7, 53, 48:16). "I have blotted out as a thick cloud, thy transgressions, and as a cloud, thy sins: return unto me; for I have redeemed thee" (Isa. 44:22). To say "have redeemed" is past tense, but when associated to events after Jesus, it becomes present tense. Therefore, Isaiah is talking about the future, a time when redemption for the believers are in force.

Through the ages God has cautioned his angels to be patient for the harvest. "Let them" (both the wheat and the tares) "grow together until the harvest" (Mt. 13:30). God's spiritual kingdom is now on earth, separating the wheat from the tares. This "marvelous" work of God has brought half the population of the world into direct association with Jesus. Today we are finding inroads being made into the more heathenistic nations of the world. Those who once rejected Christian missionaries, are now receiving shipments of Bibles. Often their christian thoughts are derived directly from the Bible. Should one choose to receive, and truly believe, God's knowledge will be added unto them (Lu. 12:30–31).

The Bible says it will be published through out all the world, and then the end shall come (Mr. 13:10). It has taken into this historical period before this prophesy could be fulfilled. But all prophesy must be fulfilled in its proper order before God continues with the next prophetic step.

The offspring with more Israelite blood, would of course, be more inclined to respond to God's spiritual message when they hear it. Should they become spiritually enlightened, and repentant, they will become a example unto other Gentiles. All may be adopted through faith (Rom. 8:15; Gal. 4:5). This was exactly the same way Joseph's two sons Ephriam and Manasseh, who themselves were half Gentile blood, were adopted into the house of Israel by their grandfather Jacob.

Jewish people have equal opportunity to be saved under grace, but as a body they still do not accept Jesus Christ. During grace the Jews are cast aside for "the reconciling of the world" (See Rom. 11:15). Paul and Peter were both commissioned to take the gospel to the Gentiles (Rom. 11:13; Jn. 10:16–17). No doubt some Jews were the first Christian converts, but as Paul indicated, the "good news" spread more rapidly among the Gentile nations.

Jesus refers to lost Israel as "My sheep" (Jn. 10:27). God's lost sheep are not lost unto him and they will hear His voice (See Ez. 34; Jn. 10:14–16). Scriptures indicate there will be a grand reunion of all Israel, Knowledge to properly identify all the lost shall be known just before the millennium. One hundred forty-four thousand, twelve thousand from each tribe, will be especially sealed (Rev. 7:5–8). This earth will then be divided into twelve different sections during God's millennium reign (See Ez. 48; Rev. 7).

During the millennium God will restore physical life to the

righteous dead, and the living will be changed (I Cor. 15:52). Jesus will take David's place as king, and rule this earth as it is done in heaven (Lu. 11:2–4). This rule by a benevolent king (God) will last for a period of one thousand years.

Abraham, his son Isaac, and Isaac's son Jacob are the great patriarchs to receive these original blessings and promises by God. Isaac was favored over Abraham's son Ishmael, Jacob was favored over Isaac's son Esau (See Mal. 1:2, Rom. 9:13). Most become confused about usurping the firstborn heritage, but let us not forget that God has said He is no respecter of persons (Acts. 10:34). God is not subject to man's whims and earthly traditions. It is God who does the choosing, and He chooses those who are touched with the spirit to carry out His will (Rom. 9:15).

God came to Jacob one evening and wrestled with him as a man (Gen. 32:24). God put down a ladder from heaven to Jacob and confirmed upon him all the blessings he had once given to Abraham (Gen. 28:12–15). God changed Jacob's name to Israel: "Thy name shall be called no more Jacob, but Israel; for as a prince hast thou power with God and with men, and hast prevailed" (Gen. 32:24–29).

In Hebrew the name Israel means "might," a "strong nation," or a "mighty people" in the Lord. We will become more and more aware how these terms apply to the lost people of Israel. Such biblical expressions are there to expose the nations where Christ like things are done. Try to become knowledgeable of Isaiah chapters 42, 43, 44, and the first six verses of chapter 45.

Before Jacob blessed his own twelve sons, his namesake "Israel" was given to his grandsons Ephraim and Menassah (Gen.

48:8–22). From that exciting moment onward, Jacob called Joseph's sons his "own." At that time Jacob was the great patriarch for all Israel. This adoption act set a president that would be used at a later time. A time when the world would be under God's coming grace. During grace, anyone can become adopted into Israel. Even the heathen can be placed along with the patriarchs Abraham, Isaac, and Jacob (Gal. 3:8). This act of adoption by Jacob is important to get to know. It is the recipe for the future disposition for faith, and the Christian pay the incident little regard. Yes, when Israel sinned, they sometimes used the incident to cover over the severity of their sinful doings.

Jesus made it possible for *all* believers, under grace, to be equally *adopted as sons*. Remember, Joseph had married into the Egyptian race. The Egyptians are descendants of Ham, whose father is Noah. Ham's family had previously received a curse from God (See Gen. 9:25–26; 10:6) All this means a a time will come when those born outside the promise may also be adopted just as Joseph's two sons were. How grace is extened to anyone who gains knowledge about Jesus. They may become part of the spiritual body of God, providing they are able to understand the significance of His physical sacrifice. This knowledge bridges the gap from the Old Testament to the New.

Jacob pronounced blessed Ephraim and Menassah to "grow into a multitude in the midst of the earth" (Gen. 48:16). In Genesis 49, Joseph is himself awarded a blessing that his descendants would become "shepherds" among Israel (Gen. 49:24). The bulk of these "shepherds" went north into captivity along with the lost ten tribes. They have also become hidden by mixing among the Gentile nations.

The descendants of Joseph are more likely to respond in earnest to the Bible message, because his lineage are those inclined to become community Pastors. They are fore told to be shepherds of the flock. Pastors are shepherding lost Israel by keeping the words of Jesus alive in the churches down through history. Other members of lost Israel are more inclined to follow the truth they hear about God. Being a blessed people, when they hear the truth, they change their demeanor to follow after Jesus. Each new follower can become an ambassador to Jesus Christ.

The Bible indicates a serious religious decline to take place at the last days. Many of the shepherds will be pushed aside as false ministers take over, even until they deny the power of godliness (See Isa. 56:10–11; II Tim. 3:5, 4:3–4). These same ministers will be against any new thoughts. A book such as this spark their ire because it has new thinking. Especially when it explodes the "once saved, always saved" theory with the adoption explanation.

Jesus preached directly to ones heart as Jeremiah once predicted (Jer. 31:33). His words brought to earth a New Covenant. A new law that is a spiritual affirmation of the old one. The old one that predates Josiah's reformation. The physical was affirmed and completed when Jesus subjected himself to be our sacrifice. The new law was the act of *love!*

Now it is Jesus who becomes our high priest (Heb. 7:21–25), instead of a priesthood passed from father to son: "Now the just shall live by faith: but if any man draw back, my soul shall have no pleasure in him" (Heb. 10:38). Try to remember the scripture just quoted. It confirms that one might "draw back" from the faith. This happens over and over again in our personal lives, just as it has happened over and over again with God's chosen people Israel.

All through the Book of Jeremiah, the prophet takes issue with the priests. He told the priests how both circumcision and sacri-

fice were in vain unless perceived with a change in their hearts (Jer.
4:4). Though Jeremiah was a powerful prophet, his words fell on
deaf ears, as the priests plotted his death (Jer. 11:18–23). God
told Jeremiah: "Backsliding Israel (northern ten tribes) hath justified herself more than treacherous Judah" (Jer. 3:11). This is God's
final gesture before He took away the national status of Judea. It
would be 1948 A.D. before they would attaint it again.

As prophesied, the Jews would never fully recover from the
treachery imposed upon them through the priests. God told
Jeremiah, "Behold, the days come saith the Lord, that I will make
a covenant with the house of Israel, and with the House of Judah:
not according to the covenant that I made with their fathers in the
day that I took them by the hand to bring them out of the land of
Egypt; which covenant they break, although I was a husband unto
them, saith the Lord; But this shall be the covenant that I shall
make after the days of Israel: After those days, saith the Lord, I will
write the Law in their inward parts, and write it in their hearts"
(Jer. 31:31–34).

Jeremiah is addressing lost Israel when he uses these words:
"Go and proclaim these words toward the north, and say: Return,
thou backsliding Israel, saith the LORD; and I will not cause mine
anger to fall upon you: for I am merciful, saith the LORD, and I
will not keep anger forever" (Jer. 3:12).

Remember, the *southern* kingdom of Judah has not yet been
destroyed by the Babylonians when Jeremiah uttered these words.
They were about to be attacked as Jeremiah had predicted, but at
the moment, Jeremiah's warnings would go unheeded by the kingdom of Judah in Jerusalem. Just as God's warnings to northern
Israel went unheeded one hundred and thirty-four years earlier.

Hilkiah had Jeremiah put into prison to stifle opposition to his sweeping religious reforms. Placed in context the Book of Deuteronomy flares against the truth of faith by stretching it to accommodate the ambitions of the priests.

Read what happened to the priests When they moved to usurp prophetic powers before (See Num. 16:16–33). "And it came to pass, as he had made an end of speaking (Num. 16:3) all these words, that the ground clave asunder that was under: And the earth opened her mouth, and swallowed them up, and their houses and all the men that appertained unto Korah (Priest in Moses day) and all their goods" (Num. 16:31–32). This destruction of the priests who tried to usurp the power of Moses is almost as dramatic as the parting of the Red Sea. Lucky for the priests that God was about to give up on Israel when they added words to the Bible and called it sanctified by Moses. Otherwise they would have been swallowed up in the earth. Hilkiah and the priests were very fortunate that God was disappointed with all Israel this time. He is still disappointed with them til this day.

The law of stoning in the Book of Deuteronomy (Deut. 4:2; 17:14–20) allowed the common people to become instant judges and executioners (Deut. 17:6, 21:21, 22:24). Yes, God did call for the stoning death of those who "hath a familiar spirit" (Lev. 20:27). God is the only one who has power over life and death. How could God stand behind the stoning death of Stephen (Acts 7:57–60)?

Deuteronomy does not wait for God to confirm stoning. It puts death in the hands of laymen and women. Three people who consort together can legally declare a general execution upon whomsoever they can inspire the mob crowd to condemn.

The Jewish detractors of Jesus often tried to trap him into a situation where he could be stoned to death. This is the type of hypocrites Jesus had to contend with. Jesus was intelligent enough to throw some of their hypocritic notions right back at the detractors. This may be why Jesus quotes a lot from the Book of Deuteronomy. It would be very hard to prosecute Jesus when He quoted from their scriptures.

The kingdom of Judah fell in 587 B.C. bvy the hands of the Assyrians. Fifty years later the Assyrians were defeated at the hands of the Babylonians. It was during those years of captivity that Daniel counted down their remaining years to glory. Daniel was puzzled over the words of Jeremiah as they were written in chapter 22, and 23. He found the Jews would be restored to their former glory, after the space of four more world ruling empires (See Dan. 2–7). Daniel could not reconcile the harsh works spoken in Jeremiah (23:11). Not if they were to anoint their most holy (Dan. 9:24).

Daniel put a time limit upon this anointing event: "Seventy weeks are determined upon thy people and upon thy holy city" (Dan. 9:24). Scholars agree that the seventy year period describes by Daniel would amount to 490 years. This time period was to begin after they returned to Jerusalem and rebuilt their temple in 537 B.C. (Dan. 9:25). Christians should know that Jesus interrupted the Jewish countdown by being "cut off" as prophesied by Daniel (Dan. 9:26).

It is strange how we all select verses from the Bible we like to hear and ignore those we do not like to hear. Daniel did not like Jeremiah's condemnation of the Jewish people when the word he received about them was so good. He did not understand, and neither have the Jews, that this time period would have to be interrupted while God gathered the lost ten tribes (Hab. 2:3).

Even the first apostles were inclined to believe that Jesus would return to culminate his work almost immediately. The constant presence of the holy ghost was new to them, but they soon adjusted, and came to realize it was going to take many generation for the work they started to be done.

We now know it has taken thousands of years for God's "marvelous work" to draw to an end. In the meantime, God's benevolent kingdom on earth still exists to fill another spiritual time gap between Daniel's 69th and 70th yearweeks.

We should never lose sight of the fact; as Daniel did not understand, that the Jews have seven more years to bring themselves into glory after the time of the Gentiles is up (Lu. 21:24). After grace for the Gentiles is over the Holy Ghost will leave the earth: "And he shall confirm the covenant with many for one week: and in the midst of the week he shall cause the sacrifice and the obligation to cease, and for the overspreading of the abominations he shall make it desolate, even until the consummation, and that determined shall be poured upon the desolate" (Dan. 9:27). Can we understand the scriptures? *There is a double ending* to this world. All within a seven year framework!

Jesus was indeed the Messiah (Jn. 4:25, 26), but He was not scheduled to perform with judgment and "vengeance" until Daniel's seventieth year-week period is over. It is delayed during our present time of grace, while the Jewish people have been dispersed, humbled, and humiliated. Today they are being assembled for their future role. That role begins with the mass acceptance of Jesus as He comes back among them to build their temple.

The Jews will appreciate Jesus when he does appear to them, because He will show them the nailprints on His hands and feet (Zech. 2:7–12; 3:8; 6:12). "And I will bring the third part through the fire, and will refine them as silver is refined, and will try them as gold is tried: they shall call on my name, and I will hear them: and they shall say, The Lord is my God" (Zech. 13:9).

When the disciples of Jesus asked Him about the end, they were told to look for the "abomination of desolation spoken by Daniel the prophet" (Mt. 24:15). The abominations mentioned by Daniel the prophet coincide with a collapse in our western world's political and economic system (See Ez. 7:19). This disaster unsettles the world until order is restored by enacting a new political system.

No, the seventieth year for the Jews has not resumed just yet. We have to wait until the "times of the Gentiles are fulfilled" (Lu. 21:24). This time comes when the world is thrown into a minor chaos by some natural event. No man alive can tell you when this even will occur. All anyone can do is be alert and always prepared (Mt. 24:44; 24:36).

When the Holy Ghost leaves this earth the clock starts ticking again for the Jewish people. Those who remain of the earth will witness a tremendous heat flash as with is goes all those worthy souls living on earth with part of the Holy Ghost connected to their souls. (See I Cor. 15:52; Isa. 30:26; Ez. 39:6).

The Jewish people will be forced to rely on Jesus in order to gain access to their genealogies. Their records were lost when their temple was destroyed by the Romans in 71 A.D. There is a remnant from each of the twelve tribes within Judaism as ancient commerce was exchanged between the north and south kingdoms. A few in the north escaped to the southern kingdom when the Assyrians attacked. In fact, one apostle accepted Jesus as the Messiah based upon the simple fact that Jesus knew he was an "Israelite" (A descendant of Joseph. See Jn. 2:46–51). Nathaniel understood his genealogy was unique among the Jews and he was impressed that Jesus was also aware of it.

Jesus came to His own because it was prophesied that the Messiah would come through the lineage of David. (II Sam. 7:13; I Chron. 17:14; II Chron. 6:16, 7:18; Ps.145:13). Jesus let it be known that: "My kingdom is not of this world" (Jn. 18:36). Jesus also said: "To this end was I born, and for this cause came I into the world" (Jn. 18:37). Again, Jesus did not come at the time to attack Satan, He came to establish His kingdom of "righteousness" on earth (Jn. 14:16–21). We all may enter this kingdom through God's grace, providing we learn to worship him in "spirit and truth" (Jn. 4:24).

Jesus was born a Jew (Jn. 7:42) but without corruption (Lu. 3:23–38). When He was not recognized by His own, He stopped their 70-year countdown to glory and started grace (Mt. 19:30). When those who do respond to God's spiritual kingdom, their change in actions does affect the lost soul. Sometimes in a way that causes tensions. "Think not that I come to send peace on earth: I come not to send peace, but a sword. For I am come to set man at variance against his father, and the daughter against her mother, and the daughter-in-law against her mother-in-law. And a man's foes shall be they of his own household" (Mt. 10:34–36).

As an all-knowing God, Jesus understands each person's genetic code and physical traits, all the way back to Adam and Eve. He knows all of our weak points, and sometimes God deliberately places things in our earthly path so that we might grow in spirit and character. Individual values need to be tested or they will remain valueless.

Scientists have discovered "DNA'" and marvel at the way it transfers the genetic code. Locked into that code are a few people with strong Israelite traits. One member of the family may have stronger Israeli traits than the other. The results may be that one child has an affinity for God more than another child. A spiritual uplifting will change the morality of a believer. This sudden mood change can bring on divisions within the same family.

Christianity in now so prevalent our western world that it has affected the social standards of most western nations.

The United States was founded upon the Christian ethic. Our Bill of Rights recognizes individual thought and personal freedoms. Christianity has leaped forward under capitalism and the new world democracies. With it has come many blessings, and many deceptions. All the more reasons why one should: "test the spirits" (1 Jn. 4:1).

It is a tattered piece of old literature indeed, but it does represent the only source we have to substantiate true spiritual values.

-MURP

Tattered as it may be, full of "stumbling blocks." often mistrans-
lated, and attacked by men of false truths (See Jer. 6:21; Rom.
11:9, 14:13; I Cor. 1:23; Rev. 2:14), and used for personal monetary gains, be ye diligent and grasp through it all, what really is.
After all this, just glean from its soiled pages the truth. There is
just no limit to its message as it unfolds the mysteries of Godliness.

PROPHECY DELAYED

Scholars say that the sixty-two weeks in Daniel 9:26 is an artificial number to bring together three periods totaling seventy weeks (See II Chron. 37:21; Lev. 26:33–35; Jer. 25:11). Few will disagree that sixty-nine of Daniel's promised seventy year-weeks ended during the lifetime of Jesus.

Scholars find that Daniel's prophetic "weeks" in the Old Testament are connected to the seven-year sabbath weeks. Daniel gave the Jews seventy more weeks (four hundred ninty years) "to finish the transgression, and to make an end to sin" (Dan. 9:24). The last year-week (seven years) has been delayed by God's ancient commitment to His "other sheep" (Jn. 10:16). Those who are the lost ones of Israel.

Yes, Jesus did claim to have finished his work on earth (See Jn. 19:30), but we should not forget there are divine judgments yet to come (Rev. 19:11). At the end of the Jewish seventieth year-week, Christ will rule the earth, and then judgments will take place. The last (Gentiles) shall be first, and the first shall be last (Jews—See Mr. 10:31).

The Jews have been in trouble ever since they concocted the book of Deuteronomy. They will continue to be cast aside until the time their seventieth year-week can be completed: "For I know the thoughts that I think toward you, saith the Lord, thoughts of peace, and not of evil, to give you an expected end" (Jer. 29:11). The Messiah will appear to the Jewish people as they expect. This is why the Jewish people have to re-assemble themselves towards the last days.

This "expected end" means *Jesus will appear to the Jews as their Messiah*, in a way they would definitely know him. The Bible tells us how He will appear. He is going to appear to the Jewish people and show them his pierced body and hands (Zach. 12:10; 13:6). This time He will not be rejected as He was be ancient Israel (1 Sam. 8:7). After this appearance the Jews will realize how their ancestors led them astray, and accept the true principles why they were asked to practice God's sacrifice.

During tribulations it is the Jews who will come to the true knowledge of their God. This will make them indifferent towards the rest of the world, and half way through the seven year tribulation period, the Jews will be depressed.

God's work among the Gentiles began at Pentecost (Acts 3:1–3) and continues until this day. In 71 A.D. the Jewish nation was conquered, just as Jesus prophesied (Mt. 24:2), and the Jewish people were then dispersed throughout the world: "And I will bring you out of the midst thereof and deliver you into the hands of strangers" (Ez. 11:9).

Daniel is more explicit when he traces the plight of the Jewish people through the history of four great world ruling empires. The fourth he described to be much more "diverse" than the other three. It is to be "devoured and brake in pieces," only to pull itself together as ten kingdoms in the last days (Dan. 7:7). This is going to happen with the eventual fall of capitalism during the last days (Ez. 7:19). Out of this collapse there will raise ten king who do much to re-establish ancient looking territories of Rome. After they come to power a man will rise up displaying wisdom along with strong political appeal who will incorporate these kingdoms into one strong worldly power with control. This prophesied event will revise the old Roman Empire as all territories become subject to this mans rulership.

Daniel refers to this man as the "little horn" (Dan. 7:8), because at first he is small compared to the ten kings. He comes to power by negotiating peace (Dan. 8:25). Very rapidly he revises the Roman Empire and casts a dictatorship over the same geographic area once ruled by ancient Rome. What happens to the American continents during this same period of time will be discussed later.

Daniel traces four world-ruling empires beginning with the Babylonian empire of his day. Daniel lived to see the second great world ruling empire, which was the Persian. The Persians defeated the Babylonians and released the Jewish population so they could return to Jerusalem from captivity in 537 B.C.

The third empire is Greece under Alexander the Great.

Rome is the fourth world ruling empire. See Dan. Ch. 2 and 7. Take another look at how the old Roman Empire will pull itself back together again at the beginnings of the seven-year tribulation period allotted for the Jews (Dan. 7:7–8); under a sinful man described in Daniel 2:31–45. This revised Roman Empire will be smashed at the end of tribulations by God, and all nations of the world will be consumed (Dan. 2:44).

Before God can "confirm the covenant" (Dan. 9:27, one year week), *the Jewish temple must be rebuilt in Jerusalem.* Jesus will return and build this temple within a matter of days (Zech. 6:12; 3:8). The world will not know about this great building feat, because chaos will have temporary severed communications in the western world. By the time order is restored, the Jewish state will be swelled with all the world's Jews who would forsake their properties and migrate home to Jerusalem, hearing by word of mouth, that their Messiah had truly come.

God's people, the Gentiles who are known by the spirit all over the world, are going to recognize the signs of coming world chaotic events (See Mt. 24:43). God does reveal the hour, but He has set the signs of the times through many prophets (Amos 3:7). This would mean from the writings of Moses (First four books of the Bible) through John the Beloved (Isa. 45:19, 48:16; Dan. 2:22). It is true that end time prophecy has it starts and delays. But this is all part of God's grand design. It is confusing: "But know this, that if the goodman of the house had known in what watch the thief would come, he would have watched, and would not have suffered his house to be broken up" (Mt. 24:43).

The Bible tells us that in the latter days the world becomes extremely wicked (2 Tim. 1:1–5; 2 Tim. 4:34), similar to the way it was before the flood (Mt. 24:37). Jesus said, "So likewise ye, when ye shall see all these things, know that it is near, even at the doors" (Mt. 24:33). We need to beware of the attitudes and trends of our neighbors. So long long as men are finding God the tribulation period will be delayed, but when evil becomes so severe that the image of God is distorted, we can expect God's wrath to come upon the world. A prelude to these times will be a sharp increase in the world's natural disasters.

Prophecy was delayed when the prophet Jonah was instructed to warn the inhabitants in Nineveh they would be destroyed in forty days. Nineveh was a heathen city, so Jonah fully expected the prophecy to happen as prescribed. When the people heard Jonah, they humbled themselves and repented in sackcloth. They threw themselves before God and begged for deliverance. God forgave them and delayed the appointed time they would be destroyed.

Nineveh changed their circumstances. As a result God changed His mind and postponed what He intended for them. The city was eventually destroyed by the Medes about 627 B.C., thus quietly carrying out God's words against them.

God told the prophet Zechariah that the Jews would "smite the shepherd" (Zech. 13:7). As predicted, Jesus became the sacrifice symbolized in the Old Testament (See Heb. 4:14, 15). The scattering of the Jewish people in 71 A.D. was predicted by Jesus (Mt. 24:2).

Thanks to their rigid *Torah*, the Jews have remained autonomous and very much together to their faith. God has been able to use the harsh and regimented Jewish law to preserve the Jewish people down through time. Now God is assembling the Jewish people to receive some long-delayed blessings. These blessings will commence when the Jewish temple is rebuilt. Until that event takes place, God is working through the human temple (See Col. 2:11–17).

Some recognize the preservation of the Bible to be a small miracle. When all religious authority became vested in the Catholic Church, many faithful humans were vicariously exterminated as they held on to what they saw as truth. There are others who die holding on to a belief that is a lie. Either way, these people are far better off in the eyes of God, for they are either hot or cold, rather than to make no decisions at all (Rev. 3:15).

Isaiah looks at our historical era, when he says: "And in that day shall the deaf hear the words of the book, and the eyes of the blind shall see out of obscurity, and out of darkness" (Isa. 29:18). But what "book" is Isaiah talking about? We are now given choices. We now have the sacred Koran and the Mormons in Utah use this very scripture to justify their Book of Mormon. Does delayed prophesy mean we would be getting a complete restoration like the Mormons say? Both the Book of Mormon and the Koran are intelligently written, but they berate Jesus (Gal. 1:6–8).

Some ministers live sinful lives, but if they preach Jesus, they may at least introduce a nonbeliever to the source of truth, and that source is Christ Jesus. If a genuine interest is sparked, no matter how one hears the word, Jesus will take it from there (Ph. 1:18). Those who do take an interest and learn will include Jesus in every facet of their lives, especially when troubled, because chastisement from the Lord is how He makes us grow (Heb. 12:6)

Observe how prophecy must be delayed by reading Isaiah the prophet in chapters 44 and 45. Isaiah 44:2–7 *assures* the lost ten tribes of Israel that God is still with them, that their offspring will still become true witnesses of God. Verse 7 explains their brighter future, and verses 8 through 20 describe how one segment of Israel will at various times be nourished by the other. Then observe how the United States watches over Israel since they were certified as a nation in 1948 A.D. Verse 21 speaks with the lost tribes after they have mixed their blood among the Gentiles. Isaiah chapter 44 leads to the day the lost ten tribes will hear the words of a book (Isa. 29:10–13). Verse 22 promises their descendants redemption. Isaiah 44, verses 23 though 27, indicate when redemption for all Israel can be expected. For Judah it starts with King Cyrus (Isa. 44:28, 45:1–4), and toward the end God will make their "crooked places straight" (45:2, when Jesus returns and builds their temple). Meanwhile, lost Israel is to receive "treasures of darkness, and hidden riches of secret places" (45:3). In other words, they shall be blessed with abundance within the nations where they dwell.

Study verse 2 in Isaiah, 44. Jacob is to become a "servant" (Shepherds) while "Jesurun" (the upright one) is the one "chosen." Surely one must agree that two segments of Israel are being addressed in this verse. Read all of Isaiah with two segments of Israel in mind to get the proper message. Isaiah was speaking somewhere between 745 and 695 B.C. The southern kingdom of the Jews will always carry the scepter promise. They are the first, and they shall become the last (Mt. 19:30), it is just that a period of grace shall interrupt the process.

When the Jews rejected Jesus, they lost their status as the chosen ones. The "chosen" ones after the time of Jesus will be his "lost sheep," or lost Israel. One really has to be careful as they follow Isaiah through the subject. One does this by remembering how the prophets speak to those under grace and those under the sacrificial law. It is sad that most theologians chose to ignore this very important distinction in Bible prophesy. Otherwise the Bible becomes very confusing and a lot of double talk.

One misses the important message of Isaiah 44 if they remain dubious to the knowledge that two segments of Israel are involved. King Cyrus cannot redeem, as stated in Isaiah 44:22. In fact, this verse reads: "I have redeemed thee." You are right; this is present tense, but it becomes future tense when it is applied to the "off-spring" of Israel. (Isa. 44:3).

All King Cyrus did was let the captured Jews go home. The text says the lost ones of Israel are "redeemed," providing they "return unto me" (Isa. 44:22). They did not have a way to return to their God until Jesus came into this world. Isaiah tell us that.

"He (God) will swallow up death in victory" (Isa. 25:8). How will he do this? "His people shall he take away from off all the earth" (Isa. 25:8).

"Off all the earth" is an expression more appropriate for those theologians who refer to the "Rapture." At that day "the dead shall be raised incorruptible, and the living shall be changed" (See I Cor. 15:52). All these verses refer to Christian believers (lost Israel) and not necessarily the Jewish people. Thus, the "many that are first shall be last; and the last shall be first" (Mt. 19:30).

We do not know the hour when God withdraws the Spirit from the earth, but when He does, the correct religion reverts back to the Old Testament covenant called "sacrifice." Since all those under grace will have "Raptured," the last shall be first to receive salvation.

There are those who call this era we now live in "the quickening." This is a good description for the erratic changes in weather and the sharp increase with earthquakes around the world. Many natural disasters will increase in the last days, like a woman giving birth.

A number of natural events, when devastating enough, could topple our shaky world capitalism.

Scientists tell us we have had some near misses recently with some rather large asteroids. The Bible tells us in Revelations Ch. 8 that we are to undergo some extreme solar activity. We are to some-day enter an asteroid belt that causes a hail of fire to hit this earth (Rev. 8:7). An asteroid is going to fall into the sea. This impact will cause a third part of all the ocean creatures to die (Rev. 8:8, 9). Another asteroid is supposed to hit the earth with such de-struction it is called "Wormwood" (Rev. 8:11).

If we become familiar with the sequence of end time events events, many of the most disastrous events take place during the tribulation years. Those who have been caught up with the Rap-ture will be able to observe these events with a good seat in the air. To those who do not make the Rapture there is still hope if one can make it to Israel and participate in their law of sacrifice. We shall find that in the final three and one half years of tribulations this independent religion of the Jews is going to irritate the "little horn who by now is in charge of the whole world. It will be very bad for the Jewish people when this man makes his move.

"But and if that evil servant shall say in his heart, my Lord delayeth his coming; and shall begin to smite his fellowservants, and to eat and drink with the drunken; the Lord of that servant shall come in a day when he looketh not for him and in an hour that he is not aware of, And shall cut him asunder, and appoint him his portion with the hypocrites: there shall be weeping and gnashing of teeth" (Mt. 24:48–51).

According to Ezekiel 7, another sign, and probably because of the catastrophes just described, the world will be thrown into a financial crisis so severe, the world is thrown beck into the barter system. Russia and China are very familiar with the barter system and would fare better than the west until a new market system is reestablished in Europe and America. Soon after the fifth angel sounds his trumpet, smoke rises out of the pit, and the sun is darkened by a star as it falls from heaven to the earth (Joel 2:10; Rev.9:2). That star could be the approach of a any huge asteroid as it comes toward earth from deep space.

Borderline Christians who remain on earth during the tribulation may hear rumors about Jesus and His activities in Jerusalem. This will be confusing to them unless they consult their Bibles and learn the truth about what is happening.

Stories about Jesus being among the Jewish people will cause a threat to the world emperor (otherwise known as the Anti-christ). He will journey to Jerusalem, where he will desecrate the temple and claim himself to be god. This event takes place mid point, three an one half years into the tribulation period. The Jewish temple has been servicing the Jews for over three years by then.

One of the evil deeds the antichrist will do is to introduce, and compel the Jews to accept, his own religion. Then he will compel all others in the world to recognize his religion, and himself as God. This religion is identified by the Apostle John in Revelations as it is compared to the old Babylonian religion. John is very explicit when he describes it as: "MYSTERY BABYLON THE GREAT, THE MOTHER OF HARLOTS AND ABOMINATIONS OF THE EARTH" (Rev. 17:5). All one has to do to recognize this new religion is to understand what the old

Babylonian was like. Satan has been trying to put it across on humanity since the world began. We will take next chapter to do it.

MYSTERY BABYLON

On his first visit to Thessalonia, Paul delivered a "rapture" message (See I Thes. 4:16–17). He explained, that those who were alive at the last day would be caught up into heaven if they had the indwelling of the Spirit. Those deemed not worthy would remain on earth to face some very perilous times.

On his second visit to Thessalonia the people were puzzled. Had they have missed the rapture, they asked? Paul assured them they had not missed the rapture. Then he gave them one important criterion to let them know whether they were living during the time of the coming tribulation: "Let no man deceive you by any means: for that day shall not come, except there come a falling away first, and that man of sin be revealed, the son of perdition" (2 Thes. 2:3). Men who remain on this earth during tribulations will be exposed to the man Daniel calls the "little horn" (See Dan. 7:8) the one John calls the antichrist (1 Jn. 2:18, 4:3), and the one whom Paul refers to as the "man of sin."

Paul's "man of sin" has become way overemphasized down through the ages. During the early church period it was applied to the Roman dictators. Nero (A.D. 54–68) was mistaken to be the "man of sin." because he mass executed Christians. Through the centuries some Christian sects have maintained that Nero was indeed the antichrist. They say we have been living in the tribulation period since his time.

Centuries of confusion about the antichrist have caused scholars and theologians alike to think Paul's "man of sin" is the first sign to look for to identify the end. The evil man has become identified with the apocryphal sign *666* found in Revelation 13:18. Actually, the *666* symbol identifies a church! Those with wisdom will recognize the sign, because it is a spiritual falling away (II Thes. 2:3).

The *666* sign is numbers that apply to a counterfeit religion. It will gain in strength before the end comes. This church will distort the image of God as it gains favor, espousing amazing fables about God (II Tim. 3:3–4).

The antichrist will gain political control during the tribulation by passing himself off as a man of peace. He acquires political power through cunning and wisdom (Daniel 8:25). John attests to the fact that an antichrist would come (Jn. 2:18), and there have been antichrists with us all down through the ages, so a more pointed sign to look for in the coming end of times would be Paul's falling away!

"And for this cause God shall send them strong delusion, that they should believe a lie" (2 Thes 2:11). This lie, or "delusion," is predicted to gain "power to give life unto the image of the beast" (Rev. 13:15). *666* is the talisman to identify the "delusion" involved at the last days.

Paul's "man of sin" will become more obvious later as we discuss the tribulation, but that evil man will not be recognized fully, until half way through the period. The "falling away" means a time will come when men and women will "not endure sound doctrine" (2 Tim. 4:3). The *666* scourge actually applies to a church that springs to the front during the latter-day Christian drought of truth.

Satan is not slack. He has been whittling away at Christianity for a good number of years now. If Christianity is going to fall away, Satan would develop a system to replace it. We can look for some counterfeit religion to make its way in this world at the last days.

It becomes strong enough to "give life," and "worship" to the coming antichrist (Rev. 13:15). This religion will develop gradually and be no big threat at first. It just grows as it waits for its opportunities. This church would need a strong base and growing base. It would gain in strength as the basic principals of Christianity become weaker. Once the antichrist is exposed, this church develops to become the "second beast" described in Revelation 13:11.

The antichrist, or Paul's "man of sin," is involved in the first three verses of Revelation 13. The antichrist cannot be identified during the first phase of tribulation, because he must first cease power from the ten world kings who have replaced our known capitalistic governmental systems when chaos occurred. For the first half of the tribulation period, both this church and the antichrist will be busy consolidating their new positions in the world. The antichrist must subdue ten kingdoms in Europe while the false religion, or "Mystery Babylon," becomes a powerful theocracy in north and south America (See Dan. 7:11–19). After three and one half years the two systems will combine as it is so adequately described in Revelation 13.

The Bible is written in a way so that it interprets itself. It enlightens men about this world's changing events. New knowledge and experiences should awaken old meaningless scriptures and give them a true value. On the other hand, some of today's conservative church organizations and individuals who claim to search for the truth simply turn their backs on truth if it does not fit their version of reality. In the last days their failure to preach sound doctrine will help alienate many to this new church.

There have always been tribulation put upon true believers since the world began. True believing Christians were slaughtered during the dark ages. Few of these survived to carry on the fact that it takes both faith and knowledge to understand our prophetic future. There has been a revival since then, but there will be a new denial of God's in the last days (II Tim. 3:5). No doubt this will be caused by a lack of discipline in the family (Isa. 3:12).

We should get to know how to read the prophet Isaiah. Most of the first part of his book is written to the lost tribes of Israel. To those whom the Lord has "hidden." Isaiah tell is this: "And he shall be for a sanctuary; but for a stone of stumbling and for a rock of offence *to both the houses of Israel,* for a gin and for a snare to the inhabitants of Jerusalem" (Isa. 8:14) Yes, God does refine all of his chosen people. "For all this his anger is not turned away, but his hand is stretched out still" (Isa. 9:12). God may bring us through the fires of His indignation but in the end He will have very capable souls.

The Rapture will go almost unnoticed because of the chaotic conditions on earth. People will be scrambling around in the world just to find food (Isa. 5:9). It will be a serious time of chaos when famines occur as the economy comes to an abrupt halt. During

this time of crisis the Russians are going to pull themselves together and make an effort to invade the United States in an half
hearted effort to take what is left of our our wealth. This will cause
minor clashes on both our coasts, but earthquakes and pestilence
will throw them back (Isa. 2:21). Owing to this series of woes, the
people around the world will not realize exactly when the saints
Rapture from off this earth. The final woe will be a heat flash
brought on by the Rapture. In some places it will scorch the earth
with 470 degree heat (Isa. 30:26). The Holy Ghost will leave this
earth at this juncture (II Thes. 2:7). Leaving with Him will be
those changed in a twinkling of an eye (II Thes. 2:7; I Cor. 15:52).
The world will be left as it was in ancient times. Again, the Jews
will become God's example to the rest of the world.

Our vast networks of communication will be in serious disarray
as our capitalistic forms of government fail in the western world
(See Ez. 7:19). Thus, during tribulation, God's kingdom is no
longer present on earth. The Jews will literally learn, by the presence
of Jesus, the way all of us should be good servants (Isa. 42).

How do we know when these perilous are close? A multitude of scriptures in the Bible show the signs of the times for
the last days.

Some are quite subtle like what we find in Isaiah 3:12: "As for
my people, children are their oppressors, and women rule over
them. O my people, they which lead thee cause thee to err, and
destroy the way of thy paths."

Look at the way our leaders in the United States Government
have wiped away some very basic and long-established moral codes.

It has become illegal to place Christian principles in public places, principles that once were the strength of this nation.

We are a nation on the decline, because we are lacking moral knowledge (See Hosea 4:6). Lack of enough knowledge to maintain the workmanship of God can be classified as part of the "falling away first." Christians today have drifted so far from what God really intended, they no longer try to expose an evil religion for what it is. This evil religion is actually a synagogue started by Satan, to coexist among them, one that gives lip service to Jesus while at the same time is diametrically opposed to what Jesus did for man.

This relatively new distortion of Christianity teaches Jesus did his real suffering in the garden of Gethsemane. Thus making God's most powerful legacy practically void.

Jesus miraculous atonement is downgraded by this church until the cross has no meaning for them. Their salvation is based upon direct obedience to their self prescribed ordinances and by-laws. They claim all power of Godliness is vested by his holy priesthood, and they are the only ones who hold that priesthood. The legal and correct name for this church is: "Church of Jesus Christ of Latter Day Saints!" Otherwise known as the "Mormons."

From generation to generation there have been miracles and signs, but as with Jesus, there is but one sign given that will allow us to know we are definitely living in the last days. Those with "wisdom" should be able to recognize the development of this religion. It is very contrary to basic Christian teachings. A religion so deceptive God found it necessary to equate it to wisdom. "Count the number of the beast," and it should culminate to the number 666 found in Revelation 13:18.

Wisdom comes from identifying what is real. Those who obtain spiritual wisdom can easily recognize the *666* talmud sign given in Revelations 13:18. The sign is associated with a religion if we check it with other signs given in the Bible. We shall see that it is a religion which actually becomes a parlimentry system of the antichrist during the years of tribulation.

Revelation 13:18 says: "...count the number of the beast," (a very simple set of instructions) "...for it is the number of a man." Simply look for a church that profanes the name of Jesus by reducing him to the status of a man.

A correct accessment of Mormonism proves they believe Jesus was only a man. As a church, their members claim they have the same authority on this earth as Jesus did: "They are they who are the church of the Firstborn. They are they into whose hands the Father has given all things. They are they who are priests and kings, who have received of his fullness, and of his glory; And are high priests of the Most High; which was after the order of Enoch, which was after the order of the Only Begotten Son. Wherefore, as it is written, they are gods, even the sons of God. Wherefore, all things are theirs, whether life or death, or things present, or things to come, all are theirs and they are Christ's, and Christ is God's" (Mormon Sacred Literature, D&C 76:54–59).

"The power and authority of the higher, or Melchizedek priesthood, is to hold the keys of all the spiritual blessing of the church. To have the privilege of receiving the mysteries of the kingdom of heaven, to have the heavens opened unto them, to commune with the general assembly and church of the Firstborn, and to enjoy the communion and presence of God the Father, and Jesus the mediator of the new covenant" (D&C 107:18–19; 76:54–59).

It is true that a variety of formulas have been proposed through the years to identify the antichrist. We propose to show you why these words identify a church, and how that church takes upon itself the many amenities of ancient Babalonia.

Jesus is no more than just an "elder brother" to a Mormon priesthood holder. At most, He was the "mediator of the new covenant," or perhaps the "messenger" of salvation (See D&C 93:8). In the Mormon scripture quoted above, Jesus is no more than a man. He was a man who can be equaled in authority by other men. To Mormons, Jesus did not even finish his work (II Nephi 29:9). He did not gather Israel.

The Bible gives us six major items that will identify "Mystery Babylon" in the last days. Mormonism has all these items, but the first item must coincide perfectly with 666?

The legal name for Mormonism is "Church of Jesus Christ of Latter Day Saints." So do just as the Bible says; literally "count the number of the beast." The total numbers involved in the Mormon name is 36. Give each number a value starting with the letter C. (Church of Jesus Christ of Latter Day Saints). C would be *1*, *h* would be *2*, *u* would be *3*, and so on until the last letter, *s* would be given a value of 36. Add each number you have valued together. The total is 666!

Mormons are aware of this formula, so they conveniently add a prefix "The" to their name. This throws off the actual count, and thus gives them a ready defense against those who try to use this formula against them. If it was just this single clue the Mormons could ignore it as a coincidence. But there are five more biblical clues that fit. For this to be a mere coincidence the odds become astronomical. First you must get the idea out of your head that 666 refers to a man. The antichrist can not be known until he appears after the tribulation period begins. Paul tells us this (II Thes. 2:3).

The second item that makes Mormonism the prime candidate is a call for a "false prophet" (Rev. 16:13, 19:20, 20:10). The Bible does not say prophetess, so this would eliminate some other minor cults. In Revelation 17, John calls the religion "MYSTERY BABYLON" (V. 5), a religion which will be greatly admired (V. 6), and started by the Devil himself (Vs. 8).

Notice in Rev. ch. 17, verse 7. how this religion is equated to a "woman," carried by the "first beast," who is the antichrist. Perhaps John make this religion out to be a woman because he cross references to Revelations 12:1. The Mormon Church does take upon itself the appearance of "Israel!" (D&C 45:1). Not only do Mormon members think they are new Israel; they believe they are supposed to "convince" the worlds Jews that they are (B.M. II Nephi 25:18).

Another item is that "*Mystery Babylon the great, the Mother of harlots and abominations of the earth*" is going to "ascend out of the bottomless pit" (Rev. 17:5–8). The Babylonians had many gods and many deities. Much has been learned today about the old Babylonian Empire as archeologists explore their ancient ruins. Archeologists have categorized as many as two thousand different names for the old Babylonian gods. These names come off ancient pillars, epitaphs, and from uncovered Babylonian writings. The big lie by Satan from the very beginning is to try to convince man that they too can become a god. Mormon members still accept and openly preach this philosophy today.

A Bible student realizes there has been false worship in the past, but what does the Bible say about Satan's ruling synagogue to come at the last days? Item (2) says it will have a false prophet. Item (3) says it must have a polytheistic deity to be like Babylon of old (More than one god). Item (4) says it must be a counterfeit Israel, not only in nature, but in deed. Item (5) says it must originate in the land God has set apart for a portion of Israel to be at rest (The United States). Item (6) says Satan himself will have to start it (Rev. 17:8).

It is to be patterned after the old Babylonian religion. This means that it would maintain temples with secret worship, operate with a divine priesthood, and worship a polytheistic deity. This church would be given authority to "causeth the earth and them which dwell therein to worship the first beast" (Rev. 13:12). As we shall see, Mormonism fits all six items perfectly.

Three other men accompanied Joseph Smith, Jr., when he established Mormonism. Each of these three men would also witness an angel. Each in turn would become scribes to Joseph Smith, Jr., when he dictated the words that now make up the *Book of Mormon*. The names of these three men are Oliver Cowdery, Martin Harris, and David Whitmer. These three men all were given reason to challenge the validity of the *Book of Mormon.* as they later broke with Joseph Smith, but none ever denied they had seen an angelic being. All remained true to that overwhelming and mysterious power that was present when the Book of Mormon was dictated to them by Joseph Smith.

Any one of these men could have scuttled Mormonism by recanting their valued testimonies. Each of these three men would eventually deny Joseph Smith as a prophet, but each in turn never denied their visions. Each did come to feel Joseph was leading his church away from some *Book of Mormon* teachings. The Book of Mormon is very subtle the was it teaches evil. Its true value plays a huge part in the first impressions of Mormonism. It is the prophesies by Joseph Smith that put Mormons on their early evil path. Mormonism is doing well now that they emphasize the Book of Mormon.

The Bible says you need only two or three witnesses to establish the truth (Mt. 18:16). In that respect Mormonism was indeed established by the required three witnesses, but what angel did they really witness? The Mormons present good evidance when they began their church (Mt. 18:16). What we need to do is examine who this message comes from? Paul gives us a test we can use: "But though we, or an angel from heaven, preach any other gospel unto you than that which we have preached unto you, let him be accursed (Gal. 1:8). The Mormon churches teach Jesus all right, but they teach him as one who has not finished his work. They claim to be a restored church blessed with the original authority to seek our and restore Israel. Jesus is nothing more than a messenger to them. He is one among many men who are destined to become Gods.

One does not find the current Mormon attitude about the plurality of gods in the *Book of Mormon*. In Mosiah 15:2–8, the deity is described as being just one God. We find another single-god argument in Alma 11:38–39. Although Mormon scriptures still confirm in some places that the Father and the Son are one God, Joseph attempted to change this by inserting the words "son of" later in I Nephi 11:18 and 11:21. In later prophecy Joseph made the Mormon God into three separate and distinct beings (See this in their Doctrine and Covenants Section 130, verse 22).

Joseph Smith present prophetic opposition to the *Book of Mormon* as he boldly and very clearly states without equivocation that David and Solomon were "justified" in practicing polygamy (See D&C 132:1–3). The *Book of Mormon* calls polygamy an "abomination" (BM Jacob 2:24–28). Joseph Smith assures all there is no hell, just three degrees of glory, by way of a great vision in the D&C Sec. #76. This he says in spite of the fact that the *Book of Mormon* says there is a hell (I Nephi 14:3–4). Conflictions like these are a part of Mormonism. They do not mind because they have a prophet to tell them which lie to believe. Their religion is much like their sacred underware. It used to fit from wrists to ankle. When it bothered them they just cut it back some.

Conflicting scriptures do not bother the mesmerized Mormon members because most have sacrificed the ability to be objective in their thoughts. They have been told when the prophet speaks the thinking has been done. Joseph Smith's power base remains strong in this area. It was used by Brigham Young to stir the Mormon migration to Utah in 1849. That which holds Mormonism together is their strong family ties. Like the Jews, Mormons like to deal with one another.

Any honest study of Mormonism must concede the fact that there was an angel present when it began. Some say the three witnesses were deluded by Joseph Smith, but the evidence proves otherwise, not when each of the three witnesses rejected him later. Their conversion was to the *Book of Mormon*, and when Joseph Smith Jr. altered some of its thoughts by inserting words, some of its early converts found it uncomfortable and left.

Many of the original church founders left when Joseph tried to establish Zion in Jackson County, Missouri. This attempt exploded a lot of prophesy as it failed miserably.

Joseph continued to add a prophetic message outside the *Book of Mormon*. His words are still held binding upon church members and are recorded in their Doctrine and Covenants. They also use old writings of Joseph that they canonized in 1880 A.D. This book is known as "Pearl of Great Price."

The mysterious *Book of Mormon*, and Joseph's own powerful charismatic abilities, are the foundation of Mormonism. Prophetic expressions for the future remain very interesting and intriguing to the members. Mormons also like to have a prophet that gives them assurance they will survive those serious things to come.

The story of Mormonism goes so deep it massages the human ego as it assures each member they can become a "god." Each person who converts to their ranks finds themselves in a congenial society that relies on each other to put it across. Without polygamy today the *Book of Mormon* far more palatable with its never ending story about good verses evil. In the Book of Mormon the good succumbs to evil.

There are other churches that claim their origin came from an angel. Others say they were established by god, but none of these has been cultured with the success the Mormons enjoy today. Though once very opposed to Christianity (P. of GP. Jos. 2:18–19), Mormons have let this attitude fade until now they are accepted with respect within the Christian communities. They excel because they are not afraid to boast about their unique doctrine. They consider their scriptures superior and twist the Bible to suit their cause. They have been told of things to come after the manner of a beautiful fable and are made to feel Mormonis will become the only religion.

The Bible warns us that "Satan himself is transformed into an angel of light" (II Cor. 11:14). Therefore it is very possible that the Mormon witnesses did indeed see an angel. Each of three men witnessed the power that was present through Joseph Smith as the Book of Mormon was translated. There men knew more than anyone else, that this power was from God, or it was the work of the devil. David Whitmer would later become ashamed of what he turned lose and wrote about it:

"I will now give you a description of the manner in which the *Book of Mormon* was translated. Joseph Smith would put the seer stone into a hat, and put his face in the hat, drawing it closely around his face to exclude the light; and in the darkness the spiritual light would shine. A piece of something resembling parchment would appear, and on that appeared the writing. One character at a time would appear, and under it was the interpretation in English. Brother Joseph would read off the English to Oliver Cowdery, who was his principal scribe and when it was written down and repeated to Brother Joseph to see if it was correct, then it would disappear, and another character with the interpretation would appear. Thus the *Book of Mormon* was translated by the gift and power of God, and not by any power of man."

"An Address to All Believers of Christ" by David Whitmer, pp. 12.

It is hard to imagine the immense power that attended the seances described above when the *Book of Mormon* came from the lips of Joseph Smith. We have people in the world today with strong extrasensory powers of the mind, but two hundred and forty thousand dictated words without retracting one word is a feat extraterrestrial indeed. No wonder Mormonism does not widely circulate this very fascinating information today. It is much to profound and mystical for a rational person to accept. The witnesses who saw this act knew it came from beyond this world. Such an association with Joseph Smith would make them ripe to see Satan as he transforms himself to become an angel of light.

Another story circulates in within Mormonism how Joseph Smith Jr. found buried golden records. From David Whitmer's story above, it appears the golden plates are there as a secondary item when the *Book of Mormon* is dictated. David Whitmer was an honest man and had no reason to lie about his part. At age 82, he was still impressed with his memory as to state: "the *Book of Mormon* was *not done* by any power of man."

Joseph Smith had very little practical education, but he had the charisma to attract the learned, both young and old. Oliver Cowdery was a schoolmaster. Martin Harris was a successful farmer. He became so enamored by Joseph's natural abilities that he sold his farm to have the *Book of Mormon* published. The work was done in Whitmer's home.

These three men were part of six who would establish the Mormon Church. They met April 6, 1830 with much nostalgia as they "voted" to make Joseph Smith Jr. its first prophet, seer, and revelator.

Seizing upon the moment, Joseph Smith took the title, and added "apostle of Jesus Christ, and elder of the church, through the will of God the Father and the grace of your Lord Jesus Christ" (D&C 21:1). "For his word ye shall receive, as if from mine own mouth, in all patience and faith" (D&C 21:5).

All three witnesses would later repudiate Joseph Smith as a prophet. Each in turn would would leave his church.

What the *Book of Mormon* does is quietly lull a weak-in-the-word Christian into the Mormon mental trap. It is written with an air of mysticism and spiritual intrigue. The story is unique the way it makes a place in the Americas for another Jewish segment of Israel. Their theme that the Indians were of Israel was popular in the 1800s.

For years Mormons tried to convert the Indian people, but today they have found more success converting Christians. In addition they have Brigham Young University extensions in places like Jerusalem. Mormon liberal arts programs have helped the State Department open up China and Russia. They constructed a temple built in East Germany long before the Berlin wall came down.

Paul cautioned all of us in Galatians 1:8, not to believe even an angel if they should "preach any other gospel unto you than that which we have preached unto." Mormons preach a Jesus, all right, but one who has *not finished His work*. (Compare II Nephi 29:9 to Jn. 19:30).

Mormons believe Jesus did not finish his work because the early church went into error after the first apostles died. Mormon members are led to believe they are now doing what Jesus and His first apostles left undone. They claim they are a restoration of the original church and vested with the true authority to spread the true gospel message in these latter days. Their underlying message is a call to gather and reestablish Israel (BM I Nephi 10:14). They now construct temples all over the world as a brisk step in that direction.

All through history Satan remains very active. He tries to counterfeit the truth every chance he gets. Early chapters in the *Book of*

Mormon suggest how the Bible is tainted by men who were interested in raising the status of their offices. The honest in heart will have to give them this point, but as we point out, the Book of Mormon is not consistent with the real way Mormons believe.

Early Mormonism tried, and by doing so, gave us a glimpse of its basic evil intentions. Men were killed when they tried to establish Zion in Jackson County, Missouri.

The *Book of Mormon* has some profound and threatening scriptures in it. Its general theme is that the end justifies the means. It opens with a story justifying a man's death (I Nephi 4:12–14). It ends with the establishment of a divine government on earth for Jesus to return to (See BM 1 Nephi 14:7). The *Book of Mormon* suggests the world should fear God's wrath and be terrified of his high sanctified ones (Mormon saints) when they do build their Zion (1 Nephi 22:14)

The Mormon religion proclaims itself to be God's only true denomination here on earth (D&C 65:2, BM II Nephi 31:21). Their ambition is to seek out those who will join with them and abide the dictates of their prophet. They gather Israel as each new convert becomes part of their group. Their vast missionary program is carried out the world over to achieve this divine commission.

Despite the setback they took with their polygamous doctrine one hundred years ago, and the stationing of an army outside of Salt Lake City, Utah, to force regulations, Mormonism has survived. Social pressure through the years has forced them to tone down their rhetoric as they mark time for the future when they expect a strong leader to guide them on to glory. Until so ordered by a future strong prophet yet to come, Mormon members are admonished to be patient until the day when they do accumulate enough control to enact a world theocracy.

Early Mormonism tried to live under a theocracy when they first came to Utah. That society was disbanded by U.S. government edicts. They were even forced to abandon the practice of polygamy. Now that Mormonism has to show a more compatible face, they have started to pass themselves off as Christians, until they fulfill the prophesy expressed in 2 Timothy 4:3–4.

Mormonism does appeal to ones basic human alter ego. They even postulate the dead. What they sell is an opportunity for everyone to become gods and goddesses (D&C 76:57, 58; 121:36; 128:8). Jesus is revered as a "messenger of salvation" (D&C 93:8), and the first to raise from the dead. Mormons feel more comfortable referring to Jesus as their protecting "elder brother." They believe this was His position in the Mormon pre-existing spirit world in Heaven. Jesus was the first born in a vast new god family.

It is Mormon philosophy that we all obtain our birth status for this world according to what valor we merit as spirits long before we all come into this life. This fable of the past continues on through this life. This life give all a chance to increase doing deeds of merit. Mormons call this the "eternal plan of progression. Failure to progress drops one into a heavenly partition void of God's celestial glory in heaven (D&C Sec. 76). There is room for progression in the life hereafter, if one accepts Mormonism there. As long as proxy work is done for them in earthly temples.

Mormons will concede they cannot exercise all the power of

their priesthood right now. They feel this is because they are restricted from living their eternal laws of polygamy.

This allows them a little lead way, or otherwise ignore some small sins, because they can not perform some commandments. Of course they can not practice polygamy, nor do government stewardships, or physical build their spiritual Zion. Being throttles back like this makes it easier to accept worldly ways and takes away some unpopular commandments (D&C 82:10).

This noncompliance has helped Mormonism to set aside some of their more radical ideas. The old idea that each star in the skies was assigned to a god allowed the imaginations of their members minds to run wild. Brigham Young, one of the first to admit practicing polygamy, tried to put a cap on such wild thinking by telling them Adam was their God, and that was all they needed to know (See J of D Vol. 1, pp 50).

A later Mormon prophet, Lorenzo Snow, still lowered church expectations with the following statement:

"As man now is, God once was; As God now is, man may become" (See Imp. Era. Vol. 12, 1909).

This cliche incubates the greater questions that used to be asked about a universe filled with Mormon gods. Today such philosophy has been abandoned until Mormons no longer know they once believed Adam was a god. They now avoid the Adam God subject because knowledge about Adam's deity comes from knowing their polygamous doctrine. Such doctrines have been set aside for so long its now dead.

Mormon people base the glory of their god upon "intelligence" while at the same time they make God out to be a genuine mystery (See D&C 93:36). Adding to the mystery is the fact that Adam is still found in their temple ceremonies engrossed in earth creating duties.

Having, and then not having, doing and then not doing, broken promises, amazing successes, tremendous failures, all seem to dissolve in the Mormon members minds as they become absorbed in other aspects within the fable of Mormonism.

While Joseph lived, he attempted to build a sanctified city with a huge temple. Today they build many small temples as they try to sanctify the whole world. Once their Zion was to be in Missouri. Now they have their sights focused towards Jerusalem.

Early members were convinced that Joseph Smith Jr. was the "mighty and strong" one the *Book of Mormon* talks about in II Nephi 3:16. When Joseph was *destroyed*, it became obvious that he was not. The church splintered after the death of Joseph, but Brigham Young kept part of it alive by taking the leadership out west under the pretext that there next "mighty and strong" one to lead the church would be an Indian prophet. Down deep they still expect another charismatic prophet endowed with the power to do the following:
"Therefore, repent ye, and humble yourselves before him, lest he shall come out in justice against you lest a remnant of the seed of Jacob" (Mormons) "shall go forth among you as a lion, and tear you in pieces, and there is none to deliver" (B of M, Mormon 5:24)

MURP

Compare how this *Book of Mormon* scripture correlates to Revelation 13:11–18:

"And he had power to give life unto the image of the beast, that the image of the beast should both speak, and cause that as many as would not worship the beast should be killed" (V. 15).

Before Mormonism incorporated itself in 1923, the legal precedent was vested in the general membership of the church. In 1923 the church wanted to borrow money from the Chase Manhattan bank in New York City. The bank was reluctant to make a fifty-million-dollar loan to an entity that needed the approval of its entire congregation. "All things shall be done by common consent in the church, by much prayer and faith, for all things you shall receive by faith. Amen" (D&C 26:2).

Since their latest articles of incorporation in 1923, the Mormon prophet no longer needs the consent of *anyone* to do legal business. In exact terms, their prophet becomes a "corporate sole." He was made "trustee in Trust," with "power, without authority or authorization from the members of said church or religious society, to grant, sell, convey, rent, mortgage, exchange, or otherwise dispose of any part of all such property" (See Articles of Incorporation of the President of the *Church of Jesus Christ of Latter Day Saints*, Secretary of the State of Utah).

This means the Mormon prophet, at the stroke of a pen, could transfer everything the church has of value to someone else. How would the general membership of the church respond to this?

Favorably, because Mormon scripture allows for such an act to take place:

"But verily, verily, I say unto you, that none else shall be appointed unto this gift" (prophetic leadership role in the Mormon Church) "except it be through him" (The current Mormon living prophet) "for if it be taken from him, he shall not have power except to appoint another in his stead" (D&C 43:4).

This momentous event has never happened before, so why did Satan put these words in Mormon scriptures? Are they there to support and help establish a religious arm for the antichrist when he does appear on the world scene? The answer is "yes," and here is the reason why.

The *Book of Mormon* decries the Bible as being distorted by dishonest and unscrupulous men: "They have done that they might pervert the right ways of the Lord" (B of M, I Nephi 13:26, 27). The overall theme contained in the *Book of Mormon* discourages the use of the Bible (See II Nephi 29:6). It contrasts with the Bible when it says Jesus *did not finish His work.* (Compare II Nephi 29:9 to Jn. 17:4). The *Book of Mormon* says it opposes all Christian churches in II Nephi 28:9–12 and proudly proclaims itself to be "the only true doctrine" (See II Nephi 31:21). What the *Book of Mormon* does in a subliminal way is to establish and nurture the very religion the antichrist will turn to once the Holy Ghost is withdrawn from the earth. By the time this happens, Satan will have the bulk of those people remaining during the tribulation brought under Mormon control.

Mormon beliefs are fundamentally geared about the latter days. They are taught there will be the time when they are to take over the United States government. Sublimely they know they are one day to gain in popularity until they have power to "convince" the Jews that Mormons are the strength of true "Israel" (See II Nephi 25:18; D&C 86:9–11). It is only they who are endowed with the holy Melchedzek priesthood. All eligible men in the church are given this divine authority by the laying on of hands. Mormonism received this power from the angel who set up their system. Their priesthood authority allows male members to confirm the Holy Ghost upon one another (D&C 20:41–43).

Mormonism's answer to man's exaltation begins when one is baptized into their religion. Exaltation comes by obeying church ordinances and covenants. The highest of these is to perform temple ordinances for themselves and the dead. They would definitely resent any temple built by the Jews. Their "New Jerusalem" is to be built at Independence Missouri (BM Ether 13:6). It is from their New Jerusalem headquarters that they intend to engulf the rest of the world.

The way Jesus died means very little to Mormons. They be-lieve each person *works out* his own salvation by doing subscribed things. They preach that Jesus did most of His suffering in the Garden of Gethsemane as he sweat droplets of blood (Lu. 22:44). To dwell in the flesh is a sacred function for Mormons because they receive a body (See D&C 93:33).

Earth's "elements" are necessary to sustain life everlasting. Raising from the dead is mere trivia to a Mormon, because both saints and sinners will do that. Thus the Mormons make their case for salvation entirely backward. "For man is spirit, the elements are eternal, and spirit and element, inseparably connected, receive a fullness of joy" (D&C 93:33). Therefore, Adam and Eve fell upward! One must become human before they can be exalted.

Physical sex is necessary to impregnate earth's "elements" into the Mormon's newborn soul. This idea holds true with the Mormon God also. They believe they need the trace elements of this earth before they can advance. Trace elements of this earth are all important, because they give eternal life to the spirit children already born in heaven. So important is the physical experience, they can obligate God: "I the Lord, am bound when ye do what I say; but when ye do not what I say, ye have no promise" (D&C 82:10).

It is very difficult for Mormon members to obligate their Lord today when they have disregarded so many of his "everlasting covenants." Once they could "enjoy communion and presence of God the Father, and Jesus the mediator" (D&C 107:19), "and without the ordination thereof, and the authority of the priesthood, the power of godliness is not manifested unto men in the flesh (D&C 84:21).

"And I will pluck up dry groves out of the midst of thee; so will I destroy the cities. And it shall come to pass that all lyings, and deceivings, and envyings, and strifes, and priestcrafts, and whoredoms, shall be done away. For it shall come to pass, saith the Father, that at that day whosoever will not repent and come unto my Beloved Son, them will I cut off from among my people. O house of Israel; And I will execute vengeance and fury upon them, even as upon the heathen, such as they have not heard. But if they will repent and hearken unto my words, and harden not their hearts, I will establish my church among them, and they shall come in unto the covenant and be numbered among this the remnant of Jacob, unto whom I have given this land" (The United States) "for their inheritance; and they shall assist my people, the remnant of Jacob, and also as many of the house of Israel as shall come, that they may build a city, which shall be called the New Jerusalem. And then shall they assist my people that they may be gathered in who are scattered upon all the face of the land, in unto the New Jerusalem" (B of M, III Nephi 21:18–24).

Joseph Smith designated Independence, Missouri, to be the spot on earth where his "New Jerusalem" was to be built (D&C 84:3). Joseph pronounced God's wrath upon those in Missouri who "hindered" the work of his saints (D&C 124:50–53).

When Joseph was forced out of the state of Missouri, he blamed the setback upon the unrighteousness of his own people. "Therefore, in consequence of the transgressions of my people, it is expedient in me that mine elders should wait for a little season for the redemption of Zion" (D&C 105:9). Mormons are still waiting for this day, but if a crisis ever arises, they have scripture like this waiting as a point to give new emphasis to their religious endeavor.

"Man was also in the beginning with God. Intelligence, or the light of truth, was not created or made, neither indeed can be" (D&C 93:29).

"Intelligence" is the label Joseph Smith used for something that has always existed according to the old Mormon polygamy story. It is a substance described as *gnloaum* in other sacred Mormon scriptures (See P of GP, Abr. 3:18). From this *gnloaum*, spirit children are shaped with physical "hands" (P of GP, Abr. 3:21), not sex, because there is no sex in the Mormon spirit world either.

Sex is an earthly function and the Mormons used to explain this in their polygamy philosophy.

To gain these physical hands, the exalted Mormon member has performed his earthly life and is now a god.

The next phase in Mormon godship is to help create a world, then populate the a new world with Adams and Eves, somewhere else in the universe. Then they fill that world with spirit children who take on bodies after they eat the wrong fruit and become human again. This enables them to have sex and thus start another populated earth.

Their eternal plan is for the human cycle to repeat over and over again. Their spirit children take that earth's "elements" and continue another eternal existence. The Adams and Eves who start that world are then made "Ahman" (god) again (See D&C 95:17; 78:16). Mormon members today know very little about all this because the story involves Mormon scriptures left dormant since they gave up polygamy in 1890.

Under polygamy Mormon's taught that "Michael" is in fact Adam (D&C 107:54). "Adam-ondi-Ahman" is a place in Missouri where Adam ascends back into heaven and again as a full-fledged god, reigns over his own offspring made in heaven spiritually and sired physically on the earth (See D&C Sec. 116)

Mormon polygamous philosophy was taught to a precious few who practiced it in the early Mormon Church. Today the whole story is no longer told. In fact polygamy was never an open discussion. Those who knew it were forbidden to tell others, just as their temple ceremony today is not for open discussion.

The higher priesthood connected to the practice of polygamy was taught in the now-defunct "school of the prophets" (See D&C 88:127). It was practiced among the highest officials of the church. When their prophet, Wilford Woodruff, decided to abandoned polygamy, as he did in 1890, no other polygamous marriages were sanctified. It did end physically, but as anyone can see, the literature remains so it can be consulted later. Meanwhile, the Mormons wait for a strong leader who can put polygamy, and things pertaining to their high priesthood into full effect.

Mormons claim their opposition in all this is "Master Mahan." (P of GP Moses 5:31). He is active throughout the universe in the full polygamous story. Satan needs help to cover all those stars in the heavens, so each is assigned a Master Mahan. For each "begotten son" there has to be a tempter. Thus Satan beguiles someone on each earth planet as he did Cain. Then that first great sinner becomes "Master Mahan", or the devils personal representative, to govern each of the many earths.

Left over from the old polygamous philosophy is the humanistic status of Jesus. Ask any practicing Mormon this question: Was Jesus created? If he is honest with his true Mormon feelings, he will answer "yes." He may not know all the reasons why he says yes, because it involves the old polygamous attitude that Jesus is nothing more than a "messenger" to that one particular world.

The old Mormon story has a lot more depth than the limited one they now teach their believers today. Their late Prophet E.T. Benson asked their membership to become familiar again with *Book of Mormon* scriptures. Perhaps he felt the time is getting short. Here is some *Book of Mormon* scripture that their prophet would like you to hear:

"...A Moses will I raise up, to deliver thy people out of the land of Egypt. But a seer will I raise up out of thy loins; and unto him will I give power to bring forth my word only, saith the Lord, but to the convincing them of my word which shall have already gone forth among them (BM II Nephi 3:10–11).

This "choice seer" the Mormon people look for will perform greater miracles than did Moses of old.

"Therefore, I will raise up unto my people a man, who shall lead them like as Moses led the children of Israel (D&C 103:16).

"And Ammon said that a seer is a revelator and a prophet also; and a gift which is greater can no man have, except he should posses the power of God" (BM Mosiah 8:16).

Mormonism's primary function must be to prepare a people to receive the coming antichrist. Those who are in it should become wise to the awfulness of your situation before end time events seal your fate. You are led by demons in a struggle against Jesus. Do not procrastinate the day of your repentance, or you could be numbered among those whose attitude might have been twisted to kill one hundred and twenty seven innocent people when their wagon train happened to travel through Utah in 1856. (See *Mountain Meadows Massacre* by Juanita Brooks).

Under the auspices of being righteous, you could be turned into a killer.

DUAL PROPHECY

At the expense of being redundant we cannot emphasize enough how important it is that we know that parts of the Bible speak with lost Israel, and part of it speaks with the lost ones of Israel. This is especially so in the books of Isaiah, Ezekiel, and Jeremiah. As far back as Samuel there are promises made that lost Israel will have to carry out if they shall come to pass. Jeremiah is called upon to explain the new religion to come which would be written in their hearts. He sees Judah scattered: "Ye have scattered my flock, and have driven them away, and have not visited them: behold, I will visit upon you the evil of your doings, saith the Lord" (Jer. 23:2). This scattering of the Jews would not happen for another 600 years. But when the Jews were scattered in 71 A.D. it is difficult to determine which prophesy is for whom.

Daniel has been excluded from the other three major prophets because he is easy to read. "But thou, O Daniel, shut up the words, and seal the book, even to the end: many shall run to and fro, and knowledge shall be increased" (Dan. 12:4). "And I heard, but I understood not: then said I, O my Lord, what shall be the end of these things? And he said, go thy way, Daniel: for the words are closed up and sealed till the time of the end" (Dan. 12:8–9).

Daniel did not understand his own prophesies because he had nothing to say to the lost ten tribes of Israel. The prophesy for them had already been revealed through the prophets Isaiah, Ezekiel, and Jeremiah. The reason Daniel was inquiring of the

Lord is that he could not understand the writings of Jeremiah regarding the seventy years of Jewish desolation (Dan. 9:2).

Daniel did not know that his prophetic four hundred and ninety years of desolation would by interrupted by grace between the sixty ninth and the seventieth year (Dan. 9:24). Though Daniel introduces the Messiah to be called "Son of man (Dan. 7:13), he does not realize what being "cut off" meant to the Jewish people (Dan. 9:26). As it turned out, the Jews chose to ignore this bit of scripture too. Christians today know that Jesus was to be sacrificed. The Jews looked for Messiah to return them to glory.

Instead of returning the Jews to glory, He extended their period of desolation by inserting grace in its place. If these old Jews had not have wrote the lost ten tribes out of there life they may have realized God had made many commitments and promises to them. The Jews were more interested in counting down the days to their own glory that they overlooked other prophesies that needed to be fulfilled.

When grace ends, Daniel's prophesies will resume for the Jewish people. Jesus tells them when that end will be (Mt. 24:15). It will be when chaos, or "abominations" begins throughout the world. Christians should become overjoyed at seeing these things because we will soon be Raptured from off this earth (I Cor. 15:52). This time of chaos will mark the end of grace, and the resumption of God' remaining commitment to the Jewish people. In defense of the Jews, some of these biblical prophesies do not clearly focus until world events move into place. This is why it would be wise to allow new learning into the main stream of biblical thought as world events occur. Anyway, the Bible does cover all this worlds events, right up till the end.

The great fable the *Book of Mormon* spells out is how a Jewish family migrates to America from Jerusalem about 600 B.C. Their sojourn in America eventually fades into evil, and the Indians we know today are a remnant who have been cursed with a skin of "blackness" (II Nephi 5:21) by God for their evil deeds. Indians today are descendants of those who destroyed the good white Indians who once built the temples and monuments found in south America. Thought abandoned by God as evil ones, the Indians are still highly regarded as direct descendants of the Jews. The Mormons are stuck with this yarn when we know today that the blood factor of Jewish people does not resemble the Indians.

We must learn to understand the meaning of biblical terms to identify the ten lost tribes of Israel who ar now in the midst of many Gentile nations. The ancient prophets called them "mountains." "hills," "ensigns," and "Jacob." Sometimes the name "Jacob" was applied to mean all Israel. More specific to Joseph's descendants we find word like, "run over the wall." Lost Israel is sometimes referred to as "Jerusalem," "Israel," "a beacon," "a mighty nation," or "a mighty people," as the loom up a majority within a nation.

Just as we recently put together dinosaur bones, we should re-evaluate the "beasts" described in Job 40:15. Prior to finding dinosaur bones no one could conceive an animal who might be large enough to drink a whole rivers (Job 40:23)

We have to wait until our present modern day before we can begin to understand the terms used by John in Rev. ch. 9. John had a terrible time describing rockets, atomic bombs, helicopters, and the rest of our modern war machinery in the language he knew. Yet we almost stagnate in old religious traditions. Actually we need to re-think and re-evaluate the Bible on a day by day basis. Let the Lord be your instructor. Let us be concerned for tomorrow and leave out molted ideas to those stuck on old musty traditions. Those who do this are open to suggestions that are based upon very old thoughts. This is how polygamy started in Mormonism. It was justified because the old patriarchs did it. Old thoughts leave you open to delusions like Mormonism "that they should believe a lie" (II Thes. 2:11). These times are prophesied to come: "For the time will come when they will not endure sound doctrine; but after their own lusts shall they heap to themselves teachers, having itching ears; and they shall turn away their ears from the truth, and shall be turned unto fables" (II Tim. 4:3–4).

Jesus said to his disciples: "How be it when he, the Spirit of truth, is come, he will guide you into all truth: for he shall not speak of himself; but whatsoever he shall hear, that shall he speak: and *he will shew* you *things to come*" (Jn. 16:13). Welcome controversial books like this to provoke thoughts. "Preach the word; he instant in season, out of season [always searching], reprove, rebuke [challenge what is being said using scripture] exhort with longsuffering and doctrine" (II Tim. 4:3). Do not base your thoughts strictly upon what other men are saying. Paul said: "Prove all things; hold fast that which is good" (I Thes. 5:21).

Our world does change, and when it does, once obscure prophesy comes into focus. A book like this could not have been written prior to the second world war. Now enough was in focus. But the world has moved so fast in the last fifty years and religious thinking remains the same. Isaiah says that our leaders will become "dumb dogs loving to slumber" (Isa. 56:10). They are slumbering as the practical sciences are the only ones who increase our knowledge. The churches have lost their position as the primary sources for truth.

Are we coming to this? "My people are destroyed for lack of

knowledge, I will also reject thee, that thou shalt be no priest to
me: seeing thou has forgotten the law of thy God, I will also forget
thy children" (Hosea 4:6). This was given to the northern ten
tribes of Israel just befor the Assyrians struck in 721 B.C. Is true
knowledge of God's work being stifled like this again today? Is
God's message becoming so encumbered it cannot reveal its proper
conclusions? Just as God predicted a flood in Noah"s day, He has
also predicted disastrous events leading finally to a refining fire.
God did not intend for his elect to be ignorant of these things, and
that is why we need to read of it by the Old Testament prophets.

Jesus told John: "Behold, I stand at the door, and knock: if any
man hear my voice, and open the door, I will come into him and
will sup with him, and he with me" (Rev. 3:20). Sup with Jesus
by reading the Bible in context. Decipher what is real from the
errors of men. Learn which scriptures relate to God's will as ap-
posed the frailties of mens wishful desires. There is one incident
recorded in the Bible that was so terrible the deed even surprised
God. Israel started practicing human sacrifice (Jer. 32:35)! Just
because it is recorded in the Bible does not make it proper.

Ezekiel uses the term "Jerusalem" as a description to identify
the lost ten tribes at one time: "Thus saith the Lord God; This is
Jerusalem: I have set it in the midst of the nations and countries
that are round about her" (Ez. 5:5). The nation of Judah remains
known, while the ten lost tribes have been hidden in the "midst of
nations," and countries "round about." See how easy it is to distinguish one from the other in the Bible when one realizes God has
not forgotten the ten tribes who are "hidden" in the midst of nations. What is harder to decipher is when the prophets speak with
first one, and then the other, as they prophesy their futures.

This is why we title this chapter "Duel Prophesy." What we
will attempt to do is walk you through the 38th chapter of Ezekiel

and show you how Ezekiel talks to both houses of Israel in this chapter. This may be difficult for those who have been taught all their lives that Old Testament prophesy has pertained to the Jews only when a good deal of it pertains to those "hidden." Hidden so well that we do not know ourselves whether we have a trace of Israelite blood. That is really not an excuse for not seeing duel prophesy in the Bible. Samuel special place in the world remains mute unless people can apply it to a place in the world. The prophesy does not reveal itself as the United States until the United States comes into existence.

From out humble beginnings the United States has progressed to become what Isaiah calls: "a beacon upon the top," or "an ensign on the hill" (Isa. 30:17; 18:3). History records that our founding fathers had deep religious convictions. Many record this deep respect for God in their journals. When at one time they almost broke up in despair, Benjamin Franklin suggested they pray. Ten days later they had our constitution.

The delegates would call this government a "Republic." Our constitution turned out to be new to the world. It was full of basic human rights. No other government to that date had laws the emancipated the common man. Our government did subjugate its laws to the people, and for being a first, Benjamin Franklin said: "if you can keep it." That is because our government is based on moral principles.

Capitalism thrives here, because in order for capitalism to work, it too must be based on moral principles. Immoral influence peddling will eventually become the demise of the capitalistic society. As we have a "falling away" in the Christian moral code, where does this leave capitalism?

Read how Isaiah describes those who came to America on the *Mayflower*. He says they were "peeled" away from among other

nations of the world (Isa. 18:2–7). We are a nation "Melted out'"
but we are also doomed to their same fate found in Isaiah chapters 18 thru 23. Isaiah is prophesying a tie in with all other
nations, like trade relations, all developed under the capitalistic
system.

Isaiah describes the pilgrims voyage to America as "ambassa-
dors" whom God "sendeth by the sea" (Isa. 18:2) There were other
attempts to settle the new world. Jamestown in Virginia, and the
Spanish conquests for gold, resulted in failures. It was the lowly
pilgrim's quest that there be expression which prevailed to form
the United States. Their quest for freedom is what became the
foundation placed under the United States Constitution. Individual rights became a deterrent for any one religion to try to
impose their ideas over the whole population.

The Ten Commandments are a good moral code, but no one
has the right to impose them on another. Most of the fine things
we have in the United States got started by religious groups in the
early days of this nation, like the schools, but now we are finding
a government that restricts religious expression in public places.
Our moral code in now deteriorating and it could very well cause
the collapse of capitalism. This would leave our government very
weak and subject to be taken over by any strong special interest
group who espouses a good moral code. One that lifts up the people
and offers them a place. Perhaps a religious theocracy?

A theocracy can be a very vicious animal toward those who
chose not to go along. Israel fell into a theocracy when they
developed the TORAH. You now know what happened to them.
They lost their homeland until 1948 A.D. Christianity became a
theocracy after the Roman empire failed. They became a terror

within all nations they influenced. If it had not been for the invasion threats from outside their influence they could have become really vicious. They had need of individual kingdoms to repel all these outside threats. But the theocracy to rise world wide in the last days, the Bible indicates that it shall take us into that battle called "Armageddon." This does not mean the fall of capitalism will bring on Armageddon. It means that its fall will accomplish a theocracy that becomes more powerful world wide than the old Roman empire. This all according to Bible prophesy.

For hundreds of years the United States has been serving as an "ensign on the mountains" to nations from afar" (Isa. 5:26). In ancient Israel each tribe had an "ensign." The "ensign" spoken of in Isaiah ch. 5 is an ensign to "all ye inhabitants of the world." Isaiah 2:2 says this ensign "shall be established in the top of the mountains." *Mountain* in Hebrew means a strong presence. That strong moral presence was to be here in the United States.

"And it shall come to pass in the last days, that the mountain of the Lord's house shall be established in the top of the mountains, and shall be exalted above the hills; and all nations shall flow unto it (Isa. 2:2). The tiny nation of Israel we know today in not revered like this says. It is not "exalted" in today's world by any means. Only the known Jewish people of the world flow unto it, while on the other hand, all nations have been flowing unto the Unites States for the last two hundred years.

As a nation of people with a high moral code, we have loomed to become a blessing upon all nations after the promises of Abraham: "And in thy seed shall all the nations of the earth be blessed" (Gen. 22:18). The United States fits this prophesy. We are indeed the "fruitful bough" described in Genesis 49:22, and then again in Ezekiel 17:33.

Ezekiel and Isaiah agree on much of the apocryphal prophesies associated with lost Israel and Judah down through the ages. Ezekiel too, was called to be a prophet to all Israel: "Son of man, I have made thee a watchman unto the house of Israel: therefore hear the word at my mouth, and gives them warning for me" (Ez. 3:17). Ezekiel describes the Battle of Armageddon in Ezekiel chapter 38, but it sure is confusing to those who do not understand duel prophesy.

Ezekiel opens chapter 38 describing a battle already happening. This first battle is not so severe as Armageddon will be, because this battle happens after the fall of capitalism and just before seven years of tribulations. Since Ezekiel speaks with all Israel he runs these to battles together because one ends grace for the Gentiles (Lu. 21:24), and the other takes all of Israel on to their glory. Verse 1, 2, and 3, tell us Russia is attaching with a weak consortium. The first 6 words in verse 4 tell us this attack will be stopped, and then this verse continues to explain Armageddon, and who the attacking force will be this time in verse 5. Notice it will be Persia, Ethiopia, and Libya, along with Gomer and Togarmah (V 6). Ezekiel continues to Verse 10 before he attempts to explain who these two attacking forces are.

Ezekiel uses the expression "Thus saith the Lord God" to separate these two attacks (Ez. 38:10; 38:14). He describes who is being attack first with words like a nation: "dwelling without walls, and having neither bars nor gates" (V 11). Such language does not pertain to the tiny nation of Israel today. They will remain on guard like they are until the world changes. Notice the reason

Ezekiel gives for the attack. All of a sudden the Russian leader has "an evil thought" (V 10). Why? "To take spoil, and to take a prey" (V 12).

When capitalism fails and the world is in chaos, Russia will think they can come to the United States and just walk in and take what they want. The failure of capitalism is going to stop all commerce. The biggest chaos will be people exhausting of food. No money, no transportation. Masses of people will roam around trying to find food. This would include the military, government officials, private industry, as all panic for food. Gold and silver will not help people in that day (Ez. 7:19; Isa. 2:20). Those who have food in that day will envied. And it will be the Mormons who have it.

Mormon members had been preparing for just such a crises for years. The own ranches, farms, food processing plants, and distribution centers throughout the world. Each family has been advised to keep available a two year supply of food. Enough so that they can take care of themselves and give to others. We will see where this plays into prophesy later.

Without spiritual understanding of the pertinent aspects of Ezekiel chapter 38, we can become very confused. as a result we have premillennial believers, mid-term millennial believers, and post millennial believers. The post millennial believers point to Revelations 20:8 where Magog is gathered to battle after Satan has been bound. They believe Armageddon will be fought in heaven. What we have is Magog being used as a general term to express a huge force directed by a strong leader. Yes, there will be a war in heaven as Satan is allowed to tempt those who lived during the one thousand year millennial period. Satan will lead his imps in that battle. A federation under the direction of the Russian leader will lead the attack on the United States, and a huge consortium will be led by the antichrist during the battle of Armageddon.

When Ezekiel runs two attacks together most theologians really do not know what to do with Ezekiel chapter 39. It is very simple. After Ezekiel describes the two battles, and earth changes leading towards the millennia, he reflects back to the aftermath of the first battle that begins in chapter 39. We know this from the way he identifies the attacking forces. Just as he open chapter 38, he identifies "Meshech and Tubal" again. We know this battle cannot be Armageddon because it takes seven months to bury the dead (Ez. 39:12).

In Ezekiel chapter 39 Israel is called back to sacrifice (V 17). The nation of Israel will be given food (V 4). They, and other nations, will burn armaments for seven years (V 9) We already know why Israel: "So the house of shall know that I am the Lord their God from that day forward (V 22). By now Israel has heard also about the destruction of God's enemies in the United States by natural causes. Floods, earthquakes, volcanos, and other natural activities may have even changed the land in some places. "Then shall they know that I am the Lord their God, which caused them to be led into captivity among the heathen: but I have gathered them unto their own land, and have left none of them any more there. Neither will I hide my face any more from them: for I have poured out my spirit upon the house of Israel, saith the Lord God (V 28; 29). This should be comforting to the Jews as they experience tribulations while there are many huge physical changes upon the earth's surface.

The way men are fooling around with the basic instincts of life, along with the peace process happening in Jerusalem, should alarm is to the fact that the end is drawing near.

The first attack comes upon a nation God has set aside with the promise that God will protect them, and that they would move no more (II Sam. 7:10). We read in Ezekiel 39 that after much destruction the United States was not occupied. Like it says in the fourth verse of Ezekiel chapter 38, that God "will turn thee back." After God did this it would take another seven years for them to gain shape to fight again.

While Ezekiel is talking about the second nation to be attacked in verses 38:8, he uses the term "mountains of Israel." In this one instance the term does apply to the modern Palestine area. Ezekiel qualifies the verse by declaring the "mountains of Israel" to be those "which have always been waste." He is giving the location *where* the battle of Armageddon will happen. It will happen "against the land" (V 18). With contrast Ezekiel describes the United States as "the desolate places that are now inhabited" (Ez. 38:12). Words to describe the United States are all found in verses ten thru thirteen. Words like: "land of unwalled villages" (V 11), and a "people gathered out of the nations, which have gotten cattle and goods" (V 12). Before this critical chapter, Ezekiel has referred to lost Israel as: "My sheep wandered through all the mountains, and upon every high hill: yea, my fleck was scattered upon all the face of the earth and none did search of seek after them (Ez. 34:6–12).

Another "Thus saith the Lord God" is found in 38:14. Verses 14, 15, and 16, describe what it will be like for the Jews *after* God stops the first attack. For a time (3 1/2 Years) "In that day when my people of Israel dwelleth safely, shalt thou not know it) The Jews will dwell in safety. That is because they are going to make a pact with the antichrist. A pact that the Lord deplores. We will see why a little later.

The second attack will be a much larger force. The Middle Eastern and Chinas nations are included (Ez. 38:5). China and others will march two hundred million into the nation of Israel, mostly to show a grand force of opposition. This will be after the antichrist makes an edict that all nation in the world join his adopted Mormon religion. Thus we will find that the battle called "Armageddon" is not to *genocide the Jews*, it will develop as a war of evil against evil. Jews will be killed, but they will not be the focus in this war. This great battle will spread around the world, threatening all humanity until God steps in and stops it.

For the sake of review, in the first attack indicates that only conventional weapons are used. The United States would become so weak under the collapse of capitalism that they could not retaliate. Russia would assemble its vast array of military hardware and just try to walk in and take over. Other european nations would just watch: "Sheba and Dedan, and the merchants of Tarshish, with all the young lions thereof, shall say unto thee, Art thou come to take spoil? hast thou gathered thy company to take a prey? to carry away silver and gold, to take away cattle and goods, to take a great spoil?" (Ez. 38:13). Our friends in Europe do nothing to help us. They just question Russia's motives.

This is for sure a double scene in Ezekiel chapter 38. The description changes again when God says "Thus saith the Lord God" in verse 14. This time the attack does come from the north. The word "north" is not used as part of the description in the first battle. In fact the first is not really a battle so much as it is a force that tries to take over the United States. The people here are going to suffer these trying times filled with earthquakes and rumbling events. Christians and non Christian alike, until the Rapture occurs. The heat from the Rapture will become the knock out blow for the Russian invaders. The people who remain in the United States will rally to a new moral system of government that the Mormons have tucked away in their scriptures (D&C Section 104).

The prophet Ezekiel explains what must be an over night crash of the worlds economic system (Ez. 7:19), and Isaiah tells us what conditions would follow (Isa. 2:21). This will cause our government to become very weak. It is at this very moment the Mormons have a prophesy that they shall take over the government. It will take a little time, but most who would be in opposition to their take over will leave with the Rapture.

The Russian people will not go into near the shock when capitalism fails. They have long been under stress. They will pull themselves together to move on the United States. Without pay our whole military complex will lose it man power as everyone in this county will forge for food, or protect what they have. Why does the United States merit this chastisement? Because "Ye turn to the right hand, and ye turn to the left" (Isa. 30:21). Yes, we have been blessed, but we turn away at that terrible day.

Then comes "the great slaughter, when towers fall" (Isa. 30:25). "Towers" denotes the great wealth built up here in the United States. From our humblest beginnings, the U.S. has become wealthy. So wealth they have lost focus on their God (Mt. 24:38–44; I Tim. 6:10).

"Gold shall not be able to deliver them in the day of the wrath of the Lord" (Ez. 7:19). This will be the day when the wrath of God is turned loose (Rev. 6:17). "Wherefore I will bring the worst of the heathen, and they shall possess their houses: I will also make the pomp of the strong to cease; and their holy places shall be defiled" (Ez.7:24). The world is in for serious devastation during these years of tribulations. Even a couple hits by asteroids (Rev. ch.8)

The "worst of the heathen?" "*Omne malum ab aquilone*" (Jer. 1:14). "Every evil comes from the north" (Huns, Goths, Visegothe, Russians, etc. God seems to use the same consortium to punish Israel all the way through biblical history. These northern nations are called Gog and Magog by Ezekiel when he opens chapter 38, but God, staying true to His promise made to a remnant of Israel, will jerk this attacking force back due to natural catastrophes, such as storms and earthquakes described in Ezekiel 39.

The final catastrophe that discourages Russia and makes them back away is the four-hundred-degree heat flash the rapture makes (See Ez. 39:6). This solar flash is not the refiner's fire spoken of in II Peter 2:10, because the heathen are still left here upon the earth (Ez. 39:28).

In that day dust will be thrown into the air from an asteroid, great volcanic eruptions, and earthquakes. The hemisphere is going to turn red with dust. The moon will turn to blood (See Rev. 8:12; Joel 2:10). Natural calamities like this will leave only one-sixth of the people alive in the United States (Ez. 39:2). So much war machinery will be abandoned here when the armies pull back it will be used as fuel for the next seven years (Ez. 39:10, 12). It will take seven months just to bury the dead (Ez. 39:12).

God says: "And I will set my glory among the heathen, and all the heathen shall see my judgment that I have executed, and my hand that I have laid upon them" (Ez. 39:21). Natural catastrophes are going to overwhelm the puny weapons the Russians bring into this war. How does one fight violent storms, earthquakes, belching volcanoes, and tidal waves with just tanks, airplanes, and helicopters?

More about the coming financial crisis is found in Isaiah 3. Notice in verse 14 that this is the beginning of God's "judgments." Already we are witnessing prophesy as stated in verse 12.

Verse 25 connects these events to a time of war: "Thy men shall fall by the sword." Verses 18 through 26 tell of some very humbling experiences people will undergo here in the United States. If civil order does break down in the U.S. as indicated, only the strongest and the most devoted organizations are going to continue.

One organization bound to fare well is the Mormon Church. Their members have been told for years to stockpile food and be ready for the last days. Their preparedness will become a very intriguing factor to others here in the United States. Chaos will alert Mormon members that it is time to gain a superior position, and they will be eager to listen to their leaders for instruction. Their sacred scripture has always been ready to serve them well in such a crisis.

Weak Christians who remain on earth during this time will become easy prey to such a forward-looking church. Mormonism will look very attractive to join, because they can point their fingers to their scriptures which explain all these horrible events. Their now-dormant scriptures are full of prophecy that will now fit the ongoing events. Members will allow themselves to be guided by the Mormon gospel that is designed to set up an earthly kingdom.

"Moreover the light of the moon shall be as the light of the sun, and the light of the sun shall be sevenfold, as the light of seven days. In the day that the Lord bindeth up the breach of his people, and healeth the stroke of their wound" (Isa. 30:26).

The "breach" that needed to be healed is the closing of God's period of grace. When grace is taken from the earth, Daniel's seventieth year-week, postponed since Pentecost, will resume for the Jewish people. The first three and one half years after resumption we will find the rise of ten powerful kings to rule for a short time (Dan. 2:41). By the midpoint in this seven-year period in time, the antichrist charms these kings into submitting to a one-world government. This includes a co-operation with the Mormon Church. Their reward is to become a state religion for the antichrist. Just like Rome accepted Christianity as a state religion in 325 A.D., that soon after developed a means of mind control.

At Pentecost the Holy Spirit fell upon just a few hundred people. One phrase used to describe this event says it was "like as of fire" (Acts 2:3). If so, think how much heat would be generated when the Holy Ghost leaves the earth, taking with Him the living and the dead to meet the returning Jesus (2 Cor. 15:52). It would be hot, so those remaining on earth can be glad it is a heat flash with little duration.

This glorious event will complete what God promised to the "offspring" of lost Israel in Isaiah 44. Those who remain on earth after this time will live through some very perilous times. They will see a western world dictatorship come to power. The old Roman Empire rises again (Dan. 7:7). Eventually the antichrist will take charge of six major continents.

"And your covenant with death shall be disannulled, and your agreement with hell shall not stand; when the overflowing scourge shall pass through, then ye shall be trodden under foot" (Isa. 28:18).

When the United States loses its greatness, the shocked nation of Israel will rush into a new alliance with the strong emerging antichrist who at first headquartered in Rome. After three and one half years the antichrist is invited into the land of Israel to help repel an attack burdened upon them by a king from the south (See Dan. 11:40). Once established in Jerusalem, the antichrist will move his headquarters there.

This move sets the stage for some terrible happenings to befall the Jewish people. They, and the rest of the western world, will be forced to accept the antichrist as God, also the Mormon religion to be the true Israel. Those who will not comply will be put to death. Since the Jewish people come under scrutiny they will flee until the city becomes almost empty of its native people. Jerusalem then is turned into Mystery Babylon, similar to its ancient counterpart in the Old Testament (II kings 17:24–30; Rev. 18:10).

There are some who think the city of Babylon is to be built again in Iraq on the same spot that it was on before, but the Bible says the old city will never rise again (See Isaiah 13:20). This mystery is cleared up when one considers that Jerusalem sinks into the same kind of evil way that Babylon of old did, especially because of the antichrist and the Mormon religion. This city is to be destroyed and replaced by another from heaven (Rev. 21:3).

It takes three and one half years for the antichrist to consolidate his power and establish himself in Jerusalem. It will take Mormonism even less time to consolidate their power and influence throughout North and South America. Communications will be restored worldwide, and the Mormon prophet will watch as a man with miraculous power takes over in Europe. His takeover greatly impresses the Mormon prophet, for they have stepped up their search for one "mighty and strong" (D & C 85:7).

Their survival to become dominant in the Americas is now an indication that they should take over the rest of the world. "And the Saints shall hardly escape, nevertheless, I, the Lord, am with them, and will come down in heaven from the presence of my Father, and consume the wicked with unquenchable fire. And behold, this is not yet, but by and by" (D & C 63:34, 35).

Are you beginning to understand why the devil set up Mormon prophecy to coincide with end-time Bible scriptures? He wanted to develop a counterfeit religion. The devil can read the Bible and must distort it. He knows that in the end times God's people will lack truth, so what Satan does through Mormonism, is to give seekers his own devilish story. One does not need to be afraid of the Mormon people right now, not until the wrath of God hits this earth. At that time the more convinced within Mormonism will be looking for Christ to receive them for their glorious works upon this earth.

As we look into Mormonism we see they even have an explanation for the coming world heat flash. Their scriptures say it was to "burn up" the wicked (D&C 64:24). Mormon prophecy will take credit for the heat flash that destroys the invading Russian armies. Such a religious similarity is going to persuade may to join them. Those who do not will immediately fall under their ridicule.

Mormon members will then look feverishly for their "choice seer." They will be impressed by the antichrist's activities in Europe. To their way of thinking, the antichrist has the power of god, because he demonstrates the same degree of success in Europe as the Mormons have in the Americas. After being convinced, the Mormon prophet bargains then capitulates to him by setting him above church authority. Those who will not go along with the Mormon prophet and their deified leader in Europe, will be sought out and killed (BM III Nephi 20:16, 17; Mormon 5:24)

Mormon success during the world in chaos will seem divine in origin. All this helps them bring order to a world being overrun by panic. Other religious organizations will fail, because they do not have the answers to explain the world mess like the Mormons do.

When chaos occurs in the Americas, the Mormon prophet becomes strong as he dusts off some of their sacred literature used long ago. They will put some of their uglier scriptures back into force. Some of this latent scripture asks for members to kill others who oppose them or die. A good reference to this effect is found in III Nephi 21:12. Confused people in the Americas will flock into the Mormon Church for their own aid and comfort. Many will convert, because it appears Mormonism is the only organization that knows what is happening. Their new power will go unopposed as they reenact polygamy, reestablish their Adam God doctrine, and start a dictatorial government.

This government system will be similar to Hitler's fascism. Once established with authority they will maintain legitimacy upon the strength of their scriptures. After three and one half years they will be almost equal in worldly power as the antichrist in Europe.

Rather than to confront the antichrist in Europe, they will negotiate. As suggested earlier, these two systems are going to merge, and when they do the antichrist desecrates the Jewish temple and declares himself to be god (II Thes. 2:4).

"Will the constitution be destroyed? No; it will be held inviolate by this (the Mormon) people; and, as Joseph Smith said, the time will come when the destiny of this nation will hang upon a single thread. At that critical juncture this people will step forth and save it from threatened destruction. It will be so" (*Journal of Discourses*, Vol. 7, pp 15, 245). Expressions like this from their founding prophet will be emphasized again as they claim a mysterious legitimacy of the Mormon Church. This, and many other Mormon scriptures now laying dormant, will persuade the ignorant to submit to Mormonism and fill them with the passion to kill and preserve as it becomes the main religion coming out of chaos in the western world.

Peter said: "For the time is come that judgment must begin at the house of God: and if it first begin with us, what shall the end be of them that obey not the gospel of God?" (I Peter 4:17). Down through the ages the theologians have taken this prophecy to mean God's judgment would start upon the Jewish people. No way! Judgment will start upon those who are living under our present period of grace.

Since Pentecost, those who accept Christ have been recognized as the churches of the world. The wheat is being separated from the tares. When Peter refers to "us" in scripture, he is talking about those who dwell with the spiritual knowledge of Christ, as founded by the first apostles (See Eph. 2:20).

Jesus told us this when he said: "But many that are first shall be last; and the last shall be first" (Mt. 19:30). If the United States has a role in God's scripture, as his precious words indicate, those seeking truth will be largely assembled here in the United States, so it stands to reason we would be hit first, and perhaps the hardest, when God is ready to bring judgments to this world.

Paul said the Jews were cast away for the "reconciling of the world" (Rom. 11:15). God's new Israel, under grace, is found within each man's repentant soul. God's church resides within the individual, and not necessarily within a building, a group, or an organization. One may become spiritually whole by seeking God out on his own. Jewish people may also obtain this, but as a whole they do not fall under the Gentile blessings. Instead, the Gentile blessings fall under the house-of-Israel blessings as they become adopted in.

The day is coming though when the Jewish people will be saved en masse. One hundred and forty-four thousand are due to be "sealed" (Rev. 7:4), but these sealings do not happen until after the Holy Ghost leaves this earth (See II Thes. 2:7). The Jews will be converted en masse at the quiet return of Jesus. He will show them His wounds on His hands and feet to identify himself (See Zach. 2:7-9; 12:10; 13:16). Jesus would not have to identify himself if he was to return in his glory. He comes quietly to the Jews and erects their temple (Zech. 6:12).

Luke said: "Jerusalem shall be trodden down of the Gentiles until the times of the Gentiles be fulfilled" (Lu. 21:24). Again, the times of the Gentiles will not end until the rapture described by Paul in I Thes. 4:16, 17 and I Cor. 15:52 do take place. Until the rapture the nation of Israel we know today will always be under some degree of a threat, not from an attack by Russia until the full end of this world, not until Jesus appears in glory and stops this final world war called Armageddon.

What prompts war between Russia and the United States is greed. We are rich, and they are not. "Riches" become the "stumbling block" of the Gentile nations at the last days (See Ez. 7:19). The demise of capitalism is going to clear the way for a worldwide computer-enhanced monetary system. Central control would be necessary to maintain such a vast worldwide system.

Could this system be the vehicle the antichrist uses to gain control of the world political systems? It Sounds very sensible today, when just fifty years ago such thinking would be considered utter nonsense. Just as many of those who lag behind in spiritual knowledge may reject outright this book as nothing but nonsense— but then, those who live by faith alone are losing badly to imaginations and the world fable of evolution and cult religions who claim they have the answers. Even now, many are asking to know, and they are getting tired of old cliches and empty answers. Right now, your children are asking to know, and they are tired of old cliches and empty answers.

THE ANTICHRIST

"Antichrist" is a term used by the Apostle John in one of his epistle (I Jn. 2:18). Both he, Daniel, and the Apostle Paul make reference to a mortal man who will one day characterize the supreme embodiment of all evil (I Jn. 2:18; II Thes. 2:3; Dan. 7:8). Anti means "contrary to," or "to be against."

A person contrary to God will one day appear in this world with spectacular evil powers. He will try to defame Jesus by setting himself up as a superior being. We have a prelude for something like this when Simon, mentioned in Acts 8:9-24, decided that he could perform on earth as the Holy Ghost. His greatest feat was to bury himself alive, claiming he would rise on the third day. It turns out that Simon never did come out of his grave. On the other hand, the coming antichrist will receive a mortal wound unto death; and his deadly wound will be healed (Rev. 13:3). Thus, Satan will use this man, just as he anciently used Simon, or perhaps even king of Tyrus (Ez. 28:2). Only this man receives the power to cheat death directly from the devil (Rev. 13:2).

We may assume this spectacular healing event will be televised around the world. Shortly after this happens the antichrist is going to declare himself to be God: "Who opposeth and exalteth himself above all that is called God, or that is worshipped" (II Thes. 2:4). Then he enters the Jewish temple and proposes a universal religion. (Mormonism)

Simon lived with the first apostles. More evil men have come since Simon, but the devastating one expected comes after the Jewish temple is rebuilt in the last days. These is no way any can know who this "man of sin" is until he begins to fill prophesy three and one half years into the tribulation period. This is when he will desecrate their temple (II Thes. 2:4)?

We laugh and joke about Satan, but the Bible respects him as being very intelligent, sly, and extremely cunning. He is clever the way he sways people and gains control of our thinking. He loves for us to accept the views of others. Some churches under his control provide that comfort.

Satan is climbing the success ladder today by breaking down the free society we have in the United States. Look at the dictatorial powers given to agencies like the EPA, drug enforcement, family services, and the IRS. Jesus showed us how to use our own good sense when confronted by problems found in our daily walk through life, but just as the Jews could accuse and throw stones on the spot, today in the United States we can be accused by an anonymous person whose sole purpose is to do nothing more than destroy their neighbors individual character.

The mind must be exercised as a prerequisite for faith. "Even so faith, if it hath not works, is dead, being alone (Jas. 2:17). The ministers of Satan like for you feel obligated to someone else—a man, a church, a pastor, an altar, or even your own personal ambitions. As long as you are on this earth, evil will probe for your weakness. Remember, Peter could not walk more than three steps on water before his earthly thoughts came back to control him. Only Jesus was endowed with continuing thoughts from above (Jn. 8:23).

The antichrist will surface out of a world thrown into upheaval and despair. He is the one John saw and depicts as being upon a "white horse" in Revelation 6:2. A white horse symbolizes peace in the Bible. He will come to power, convincing the world he is a man of peace (See Dan. 8:24).

The Red horse in 6:4 is Mormonism, also called the "second beast" in Revelation 13:11. The black horse in Revelation 6:5 describes the commerce of a world-ruling empire, and the pale horse of Revelation 6:6 represents human slaughter and tyranny toward the end. The rest of chapter six lays out events to happen during the seven year tribulation period.

The antichrist will become obvious after he gains control of the ten ruling kingdoms that have taken over after capitalism has expired (Dan. 2:42). While doing this he will be headquartered in Rome (Rev. 17:9). The "seven heads" found in Revelation 17:9 are the seven hills the city of Rome sits upon. This leads some to believe the Catholic Pope will become the antichrist. Actually the Catholic will fall apart because they cannot explain these times. One of ten kingdoms will surely be north America, and we have already showed the close association they will have with the antichrist. This will help to set the antichrist up as Mormons accept him as their "choice seer."

The Mormon Church will step forward with all the prophetic answers to placate to the world what is happening. Other Christian religions will melt and give way to Mormonism because they no longer have the spirit within them. It leaves the earth at the beginning of these woes.

We see this same pattern with ancient Israel. About the time when everyone is smug about being saved, they seem to come under God's wrath. This time when wrath comes the leadership of Mormonism will remain whole, stable, and aggressive. Being unhindered and enthused about world events, the Mormon organization will triumph and remain smooth-functioning. It has enough worldwide connections to survive on a national scale. Their organization will look very attractive to the antichrist as they offer to submit all authority to him. The Mormons will champion the antichrist as their most high god, looked for from their very beginnings.

The antichrist does not make his religious move on the world until after he arrives in Jerusalem. He is welcomed there at first as a defender because he has a peace pact with the Jews. The jews become threatened at about the midpoint of the tribulations by a king in the south (Dan. 11:40), and the antichrist comes in to repel that attack. Then he just stays there to govern the whole world and do his religious thing.

The antichrist will demonstrate great cunning and wisdom. He will pull a dislocated world back into political harmony and replace capitalism with a closed monetary system under one vast central computer control.

"And in the latter time of their kingdom, when the transgressors are come to the full, a king of fierce countenance, and understanding dark sentences, shall stand up, And his power shall be mighty, but not by his own power: and he shall destroy wonderfully, and shall prosper, and practice, and shall destroy the might and the holy people. And through his policy also he shall cause craft to prosper in his hand; and he shall magnify himself in his heart, and by peace shall destroy many." (Dan. 8:23-25).

If we allow him access, Satan can control our human bodies (See Ez. 28). "Blasphemies and great power will be given unto him" (See Rev. 13:5). He will call down fire from heaven "on the earth in the sight of men" (Rev. 13:13). Performing great miracles is what allows him to be accepted as a religious leader (Rev. 13:3).

The plight of this evil leader is first discussed in scripture by the prophet Daniel. He depicts him as one who subdues a ten-king federation that rises out of chaos in Europe (See Dan. 7:7). He is the "little horn" that plucks up three of these kings "by the roots." "In this horn were eyes like the eyes of man, and a mouth speaking great things" (Dan. 7:8). He is going to be an extremely intelligent man. In just three and one half years this man is going to establish a world empire. He will restore the world back to the grandeur it had before chaos developed. It will all be made to operate under one man's control. The wealth of the world will be spread more evenly. Everyone will be made to cooperate. He will devour kingdoms by his tremendous wisdom and verbal persuasion.

Mormon missionary efficiency in America's is already helping them to gain enough people to manage a theocracy. With mutual respect they will then accept the antichrist as their "choice seer." In fact, the antichrist will become Jesus Christ to the Mormon membership (See B M Mosiah 8:15-17).

By manipulation and cunning this man will eventually control the same land mass that once comprised the old Roman Empire. Thus the forth great empire seen by Daniel, which was "devoured" and "stamped," does rise again (Dan. 7:7); first as "ten horns," or ten kings who will capitulate to the antichrist. He becomes like a Roman Caesar, the way he puts Europe back together in an empire status. Bear in mind that the United States *was not* part of that empire. This leaves room for the Mormon Church to take over North and South America.

Mormons are confident that these spectacular world events will vilify them in their pursuit to become prominent in the world. They will explode with new members as they ease their terrified minds with a religion that explains how they are now to advance with unity. What the Mormon Church will do in the end includes delivering their constituency over to the antichrist.

Mormons claim their membership is what constitutes the acceptable Zion in the world at the last days. This religious attitude is going to cause special hardships on the Jewish people. The Jews have a family religion just as passionate and personal as Mormonism. When Mormonism is imposed upon the Jews in Jerusalem, crazed Mormon members will intimidate or otherwise kill those Jews they cannot "convince" (See B of M. II Nephi 25:18; III Nephi 21:12; Mormon 5:24).

These forecasted Mormon events to come all relate to the Bible tribulation period, enough to gain notice for what they do in Bible scripture (See Rev. 13:15; 16:13; 19:20; 20:10).

If the Jews heed the advice of Jesus, who will come among them during the first three and one half years of tribulation (Zech. 12:10; 13:6), they will flee Jerusalem (Mt. 24:16-22). The antichrist will move his headquarters to Jerusalem and desecrate the Jewish temple. Then the holocaust will begin again on the Jewish people. This time they will recognize the evil about to come on upon them. A great missionary work for the Jews begun by Jesus in Revelations 7 will dwindle, because those who do not accept the antichrist will be put to death. Converted-to-Jesus Jews will come to understand their fate and "flee into the mountains" (Mt. 24:16).

Mass opposition to the antichrist will spark the battle called "Armageddon." It also invites the end of an earth era as we know it. Jesus stands on top of the Mount of Olives in glory and splits the the city asunder (Zech. 14:4). This great act stops the invading armies, and all evil is thrown into the bottomless pit. Into that same pit goes the antichrist along with the false Mormon prophet.

This final act depicts Jesus as the Jews expected him two thousand years ago. With an outstretched hand he will "disannul" the Jewish "agreement with hell" (See Isa. 28:18). A New Jerusalem comes down from heaven (Rev. 21:2), and God starts His millennial reign.

"And he opened his mouth in blasphemy against God, to blaspheme his name, and his tabernacle, and them that dwell in heaven" (Rev. 13:6).

The antichrist will employ the full weight of Mormon theology to replace all foreign religious thoughts, "...and think to change times and laws: and they will be given into his hand until time and times and the dividing time" (Dan. 7:25). The "dividing time" marks the half way point in Daniel's seventith year week (See Rev. 13:5; Dan. 9:27).

"For the ships of Chittim shall come against him:" (Chittim is an ancient Bible name for Rome) "therefore he shall be grieved, and return, and have indignation against the holy covenant. So shall he do; he shall even return, and have intelligence with them that forsake the holy covenant. (the Jewish people)

"And arms shall stand on his part, and they shall pollute the sanctuary of strength, and shall take away the daily sacrifice, and they shall place the abomination that maketh desolate.

"And such as do wickedly against the covenant shall he corrupt by flatteries: but the people that do know their God shall be strong, and do exploits.

"And they that understand among the people shall instruct many: yet they shall fall by the sword, and by flame, by captivity, and by spoil, many days.

"Now when they shall fall, they shall be holpen with a little help: by many shall cleave to them with flatteries.

"And some of them of understanding shall fail to try them, and to purge, and to make them white, even to the time of the end: because it is yet for a time appointed.

"And the king shall do according to his will; and he shall exalt himself, and magnify himself above every god, and shall speak marvelous things against the God of gods, and shall prosper till the indignation be accomplished: for that is determined shall be done.

"Neither shall he regard the God of his fathers, nor the desire of woman, nor regard any god: for he shall magnify himself above all.

"But in his estate shall he honour the God of forces: and a god who his fathers knew not shall he honour with gold, and silver, and with precious stones, and pleasant things.

"Thus shall he do in the most strong holds with a strange god, whom he shall acknowledge and increase with glory: and he shall cause them to rule over many, and shall divide the land for gain" (Daniel 11:30-39).

The antichrist "pollutes the sanctuary," does "wickedly against the "covenant" (Israel's peace pact with the antichrist), and takes away "the daily sacrifice." Many shall die. Jewish people "will fall by the sword," be "purged," "even to the time of the end."

Like ancient Babylon, the city will become a "burden" to the whole world in the last days (Isa. 13:1). Jerusalem will fulfill that prophecy in Isaiah where it says: "They come from a far country, from the end of heaven, even the Lord, and the weapons of his indignation, to destroy the whole land" (Isa. 13:5).

If the Jews heed the advice of Jesus, who will come among them during the first three and one half years of their tribulation (Zech. 12:10; 13:16), they will flee Jerusalem (Mt. 24:16-22). After the antichrist desecrates the Jewish temple and moves his headquarters to Jerusalem, the holocaust will begin again on the Jewish people. The antichrist and the false prophet will seek out the Jewish people and try to kill them. Jesus has already warned them when they see the abominations of Daniel the prophet, they should flee (Mt. 24:15-22). The big sign will be desecration of their temple.

While the antichrist dictates from Jerusalem, the city will become evil, like Babylon of old. The dictatorial powers coming out of Jerusalem are going to awaken other nations of the world like China, Russia, and India, nations who join together and march a huge army into the Valley of Megiddo about twenty miles southeast of Haifa. This show of force is going to ignite the battle called Armageddon. The result of this battle ends life on this earth as we know it.

Jesus stands on top of the Mount of Olives and splits the city asunder (Zech. 14:4). In this final act of earthly glory Jesus stops the slaughter. At this time thousands of God's saints will appear (Jude 1:14), and the millennium begins.

The overspreading of abominations found in Daniel 9:27 develops because the antichrist pushes his evil religion upon the nonbelieving eastern nations. Satan has always used the same old tools found in Mormonism, since the beginning of this world. This is why Mormonism parallels "Babylon" so exactly as a religion. It has a countless number of gods, temples, priesthoods, epitaphs, and rituals that the old Babylonian religion displayed.

Any cult that follows a strong central human figure is a kin of the many Satanic deceptions and religious synagogues. Satan's pattern of deception always remains the same. It has been successful. More recently it has been demonstrated by Saddam Hussein, Hitler, Jim Jone's People's Temple, Indian gurus, the Zodiac, just to name a few. Satan builds these ministries to deceive, but most deceptive of them all is the role of Mormonism. Satan has planned this one well, because he really intends to cheat many souls with it in the end.

Mormonism is both bold and broad enough to wrap around all the evil religious thoughts Satan has contrived on this earth. Moslems and Hindus have the numbers, but they Lack in parliamentary control. When world chaos strikes, Christianity will self-destruct, while the Mormon religion will come to the front because they supply answers to what is happening.

Much about Mormonism is very successful today because of their sly, and peaceful social image. Right now the church waits as the world's evil mounts and comes back to them. Once they *could not* get away with practicing the details of their religion, but the coming chaos will render the situation ripe for them to go back to old practices like polygamy and blood sacrifices.

As earthly religions and business successes go, Mormonism is aspiring to become one of the world's best. When the antichrist is looked to as the "choice seer," Mormonism is well on its way to becoming the dominant and dictatorial deception Satan has always wanted among men. As an evil religion they thrive best when there are adversities.

The world's population has become transit in the last two hundred years. It is now impossible to determine exactly which region on earth the antichrist might come from. His lineage comes out of the old Greek empire established by Alexander the Great.

We find this information in Daniel 8. The four notable kingdoms mentioned in verse 22 are the four generals who took over the Greek empire after Alexander the Great died. It will be from the family line of one of these generals that the antichrist springs (Dan. 8:9), more specifically from the general who pushed "south, and toward the east, and toward the pleasant land."

The antichrist may be alive on earth right now, but there will be no way to identify him until he actually performs as the Bible outlines. Therefore, we must wait for harsh world events that will put a focus upon him. It appears that those natural catastrophes could happen just as they are described in the Bible—*and very soon*!

Some who hold religious traditions dating way back to the councils of Nicene in 325 A.D. have to ignore a lot of Bible prophecy, scriptures that are coming into focus today. It is difficult to make any progress if one abides the traditions of man.

Imagine if a strange man would come into a Sunday congregation and suddenly recite prophetic scripture to those assembled. He would be shouted down if his prophecy did not follow what was generally accepted. Most congregations have a figurehead of authority. They would not accept anything new from authorized channels, not from some stranger. This is why traditions don't work and tend to disarm and defray people from acting and thinking for themselves.

Tradition become a part of us, just like a habit. Look what happened to Jesus when he tried to tell a congregation something new (Lu 4:18). To know God does make one free.

Mormonism will survive chaos, because it is a progressive religion with an active eye toward the future. They often quote Amos 3:7, because they have a prophet to interpret. "Surely the Lord God will do nothing, but he revealeth his secret unto his servants the prophets."

Should times become tough, the more members tend to rely upon their living prophet. Christianity in the other hand, has little regard for the future, perhaps because most attempt to view the future with old thoughts and a unassuming mind. Todays old traditional religions are unable to explain the future, so they cover it up by refusing to talk about it. Those who have been inspired to push forward are forced to do it on their own.

ARMAGEDDON

The battle of Armageddon will draw together an army of two hundred million men. Invaders will march into the land of Israel as a show of indignant protest of the new and universal religious edicts directed by the antichrist.

China will join with Russia this time, along with the nations of Persia, Libya, Ethiopia, Gomer, and the "house of Togarmah" (Ez. 38:5,6). This is a rejuvenated Russia after being "turned back" from her attack upon the United States seven years earlier (Ez. 38:4).

Although the land of Israel is where the great armies assemble to attack, the war's magnitude is expanded to jeopardize the whole world. Armageddon is the grand apocalyptic scene that declares a final destruction upon all humanity in the flesh. It will start at the "valley-plain of Megiddo" (II Chron. 35:22) in Israel, twenty two miles south of Haifa. The "land" in which this battle begins is a land "that is brought back from the sword" (Ez. 38:8). The Palestine area has been overrun by the Babylonians, Persians, Greece, Romans, Huns, etc. As a land it has been fought for and won over and over again.

"Thou shalt ascend and come like a storm, thou shalt be like a cloud to cover the land, thou, and all thy bands" (Ez. 38:9). The tiny nation of Israel is already a focal point for three major world religions. It is logical that a war that includes a new religious connotation might start from the Palestine area. This is why Armageddon will be fought. There will be another earthbound religion established for all the world coming from Jerusalem. It will be declared by the antichrist half way through the tribulation period. At that time it will be made compulsory as the antichrist requires everybody on earth to join. Such a declaration is not going to set well with nations like China, Russia, nor India. Moslems within those nations will become very emotional.

The prophet Zephaniah writes about Israel during their tribulation period, when God would "consume all things," "And them that are turned back from the Lord; and those that have not sought the Lord, nor inquired for him" (Zep. 1:1-6). "Neither their silver nor their gold shall be able to deliver them in the day of God's wrath" (Zep. 1:18; Ez. 7:19).

The term *Baal* is used in verse 4 to show what religious conditions will be like on earth during this time. "Chemarims" will be in control after the manner of the old Babylonian priests (Mormon Priesthood)).

Zephaniah uses the noun "Malcham" in verse 5 to describe a person similar to the antichrist. The strange wearing apparel mentioned in verse 8 is similar to the Mormon sacred underwear. The term "Maktesh" used in verse 11 describes merchants; agreeing that Jerusalem will become a great merchant city of the world in the last days.

God tells Zephaniah how he is going to eliminate this evil in verses 14 through 18. Notice how well these words correlate to those found in Ezekiel 38:20. Again we have the Bible interpreting itself by relating one scripture to the other. By putting the Book of Zephaniah together with Ezekiel 7 and 38, then adding words from other prophets, and a firm foundation is placed under events which occur just before Armageddon is fought.

The battle of Armageddon in going to leave Jerusalem completely destroyed (See Rev. 18:8). Other cities of great importance around the world will be hit by hydrogen bombs too. Deadly radiation will become so acute in the world that all flesh would die if Jesus did not end this war (Mt. 24:22).

At Jesus' glorious return the antichrist and the false prophet will be cast into a lake of fire (Rev. 19:20). Satan is bound (Rev. 20:2), and the ruined city of Jerusalem is replaced by a holy city that descends to earth from heaven (Rev. 21:2). Those who were raptured into heaven seven years earlier, along with all the dead in the past who found favor with Christ, will return to this earth as heavenly hosts (See Jude 1:14).

Ezekiel 38:8 tells us *where* Armageddon begins. Just as he tells us *where* the earlier *conflict* will begin in Ezekiel 38:10-13. Exactly *when* the first conflict begins is not known. Not even by the angels in heaven (Mt. 24:36). Should anyone fix a date when the *conflict before armageddon* begins they should be ignored. It will come in Gods's due time.

Those who are not ready for salvation will remain to experience this earth's seven years of tribulations. Many will have to prove themselves by starving to death. This may happen because the antichrist will start an economic system that excludes those who are not loyal to him: "And that no man might by or sell, save he that had the mark, or the name of the beast, or the number of his name (Rev. 13:17). Who has the power to police such a vast bureaucracy? Mormon priesthood members (Rev. 13:15)!

Immediately after the rapture, there will be three and one half years: "when my people of Israel dwelleth safely" (Ez. 38:14). Israel's old enemies will remain quiescent while the rest of the western world will undergo political changes. It takes time for the antichrist to consolidate his power (3½ yrs.). The desecration of the Jewish temple is when he goes for the ultimate title. The title of God ruling over the earth. During the first 3½ years there will be much terror followed by adjustments. The Jewish people in the world will find their way home to Palestine to check out rumors that their Messiah has finally come.

This early trauma will cause people to want to congregate with one an other for protection. This is when one can expect a mormon missionary on every block. Their message will seem to fit this awful situation. They will bring condolence. They will be the most organized within the communities. People will praise them on as they take over the United States Government.

During the tribulation days Moslems may find a new kinship with the Jews. Each will suffer the same types of hardships. They too will resist the multiple gods concept of Mormonism. Moslems will have a great come down during the economic crash. They will make up small bands of people.

Mormonism impresses their members to consider their church the *new zion* for the last days (See D&C 97:21). They expect to force all in the world to join them. These harsh measures are what is going to force the war of Armageddon.

"And Satan shall be bound, that he shall have no place in the hearts of the children of men." (Mormons will think the antichrist binds Satan) "And at that day, when I shall come in my glory" (The antichrist) shall the parable be fulfilled which I spake concerning the ten virgins. For they that are wise and have received the truth, and have taken the Holy Spirit for their guide, and have not been deceived verily I say unto you, they shall not be hewn down and cast into the fire, but shall abide the day" (D&C 45:55-57).

"And it shall be called the New Jerusalem, a land of peace, a city of refuge, a place of safety for the saints of the Most High God; And the glory of the Lord shall be there, and the terror of the Lord also shall be there, insomuch that the wicked will not come into it, and it shall be called Zion.

And it shall come to pass among the wicked, that every man that will not take his sword against his neighbor must needs flee unto Zion for Safety. And there shall be gathered unto it out of every nation under heaven; and it shall not be at war one with another. And it shall be said among the wicked: Let us not go up to battle against Zion, for the inhabitants of Zion are terrible; wherefore we cannot stand.

"And it shall come to pass that the righteous shall be gathered out from among all nations, and shall come to Zion, singing with songs of everlasting joy.

"And now I say unto you, keep these things from going abroad unto the world until it is expedient in me, that ye may accomplish this work in the eyes of the people, and in the eyes of your enemies, that they may not know your works until ye have accomplished the thing which I have commanded you; that when they shall know it, that they nay consider these things. For when the Lord shall appear, he shall be terrible unto them, that fear may seize upon them, and they shall stand afar off and tremble. And all nations shall be afraid because of the terror of the Lord, and the power of his might. Even so. Amen (D&C 45:66-75).

There you have it in Mormon sacred scripture. After the antichrist appears, he shall be "terrible unto them." In other words, when the Mormon Zion is established anyone, other than a Mormon is to be killed. That is what their Book of Mormon says (Mormon 5:24). We are fortunate they are few in numbers right now.

Since the Mormons were rebuffed in their try to establish Zion in Jackson County Missouri back in 1835, they have now turned their new eye toward Jerusalem.

Notice from these Mormon scriptures how their Jesus wants them to be sly the way they keep their world ending project of Zion-building to themselves. Mormon scriptures are designed to raise the passions of their members in times of chaos. Just as they once did in 1830's. Another incident of their killing passion is the "Mountain Meadows Massacre" in Utah in 1856. The Mormons have their eye on Jerusalem as a conquest; to convince the Jews (II Nephi 25:18). Their Zion in Jerusalem will overshadow the one the could not build at Jackson County Missouri.

Mormon people will rejoice at the opportunity to take over in Jerusalem. It will be done when they convince the antichrist. That union will give Mormons their coveted authority to reign worldwide, unimpeded by any other religious or political force. The Mormon membership will truly seem inspired to do their devilish acts. Inspired at the suggestion of the antichrist because Mormon will be convinced he is their expected super "seer" to come (D&C 85:7). "And thus, with sword and by bloodshed the inhabitants of the earth shall mourn; and with famine, and plague, and earthquake, and the thunder of heaven, and the fierce and vivid lightning also, shall the inhabitants of the earth be made to feel the wrath, and indignation, and chastening hand of an Almighty God, until the consumption decreed hath made a full end of all nations; That the cry of the saints, and the blood of the saints, shall cease to come up unto the ears of the Lord of Sabaoth, from the earth to be avenged of their enemies. Wherefore, stand ye in holy places, and be not moved, until the day of the Lord come; for behold, it cometh quickly, saith the Lord" (D&C 87:6-8). If that does not scare you just reading it, think what it will be like living through it. But this is not their best: "Behold, now it is called today until the coming of the Son of Man, and verily it is a day for the tithing of my people; for he that is tithed shall not be burned at his coming" (D&C 64:23). One has to admire Satan the way he has set his church up. Satan, through Mormonism, has even an answer for the heat flash that remains for a few seconds after the Rapture. Those left on earth are the righteous ones. This is the Mormon answer for the disappearing ones.

The first return by Jesus will be to the Jews in the manner He left. "And when he had spoken these things, while they beheld, he was taken up; and a cloud received him out of their sight" (Acts 1:9) This fact is seldom mentioned by present day theologians because it does not fit the glorious return they look for. Quietly He will return and assist the Jews in building their temple (Zech. 6:12). The Jews will observe his pierced hands and feet (See Zach. 12:10; 13:6).

Most will come to understand that Jesus *is* their true Messiah, that it is he who came to earth some two thousand years ago. Many Jews alive at that day are going to see and understand as Thomas did. There will be weeping of great joy as they accept Jesus as their Father God. A few will still reject Him because He does not offer immediate glorification. Lack of knowledge and personal gratification will do them in.

The activities of Jesus in Jerusalem *is not* going to go completely unnoticed in the rest of the world. Rumors about Jesus in Jerusalem aggravates the antichrist until the day he enters the Jewish temple and declares himself to be God.

During his run on worldly power a deal will have been struck between the antichrist and the Mormon prophet. He then replaces the Jewish temple ceremony with the ceremony the Mormon Church uses. At this same time the antichrist declares himself to be God. This ceremony happens at mid point in the tribulation period.

One-third of the Jewish population is going to survive these terrible times (Zech. 13:9). Seven years earlier the Gentiles suffered much sharper losses (Ez. 39:2). Hundreds of thousands, perhaps millions of Jews, will come "through the fire, and will refine them as silver is refined, and will try them as gold is tried: they shall call on my name, and I will hear I will say, It is my people: and they shall say. The Lord is my God (Zech. 13:9).

The Bible tells us that those receptive to the spirit during the tribulation period will be attended by angels from heaven (Rev. 14:6). A clear indication that the spirit will function during tribulations as it did in the Old Testament.

Revelation 21:2 confirms that a whole new city of Jerusalem will come down from heaven. This event ushers in the millennium when God will rule on earth, as it is done in heaven (See Isa. 65:15-25; Jude 1:14). At that time those who were "meek shall inherit the earth" (Mt. 5:5). The prophets Ezekiel (Ch, 48), Isaiah (Ch, 66), and John (Rev. 7) talk about the way this world will be sectioned off into twelve districts when God dwells over this earth.

"The wolf also shall dwell with the lamb, and the leopard shall lie down with the kid; and the calf and the young lion and the fatling together; and a little child shall lead them.

"And the cow and the bear shall feed; their young ones shall lie down together; and the lion shall eat straw like the ox.

"And the sucking child shall play on the hole of the asp, and the weaned child shall put his hand on the cockatrice den.

"They shall not hurt nor destroy in all my holy mountain: for the earth shall be full of the knowledge of the Lord, as the waters cover the sea" (Isa. 11:6-9).

After one thousand years of divine rule by Jesus, Satan will be "loosed" for a while. This will be the final gathering of the evil ones and the last time they will ever see God. Each will bow their knee to Jesus as they accept the disposition of their final fate (Rom. 14:11).

Adam and Eve originally sinned under ideal conditions. Others will do likewise during the millennia reign of Jesus Christ, but all shall be judged at the final "white throne" judgment (Rev. 20:11). Those judged to be wicked are destroyed in the all-consuming fire mentioned in II Peter, 3:10. This fire consumes the whole universe—the sun, moon, stars, planets, asteroids, comets, everything (Rev. 20:7-10). Those who have endured, and have been accepted by, Christ will be given new bodies for the new age to come (Mt. 19:4; Mr. 12:25). Theyshall come with "full of the knowledge of the Lord" (Isa. 11:9).

Eternity is achieved when each individual is allowed to partake of the tree of life. The same tree that was once in the garden of Eden, but now it resides in God's paradise (Rev. 22:14). God determines whose names are written in the Book of Life (Rev. 3:5), and who is eligible to partake of understand the significance of what this meant for the rest of us. the tree (Isa. 29:16; Rom. 9:15). They will be those who confess that God became flesh (I Jn. 4:3), and will know all the particulars.

The flesh of Jesus was lifted up. So will ours be for the millennium, but when all material substances are burned, we will be given new bodies for our eternal heavenly mansion. We will have our sins wiped away and our new bodies will be perfected (See Rev. 22:2; Gen. 3:24; Isa. 65:17; II Peter 3:13).

The Battle of Armageddon will be stopped when Jesus displays his Godly glory. This completes God's promise to the Jews when He vowed to "disannul" the Jewish agreement with "hell" (Isa. 28:18). God's glorious appearance will be like "lightning cometh out of the east, and shineth even unto the west" (Mt. 24:27); "And his feet shall stand in that day upon the mount of Olives, which is before Jerusalem on the east, and the mount of Olives shall cleave in the midst thereof toward the east and toward the west, and there shall be a very great valley; and half of the mountain shall remove toward the north, and half of it toward the south" (Zech. 14:4).

"When the unclean spirit is gone out of man, he walketh through dry places, seeking rest; and finding none, he saith, I will return unto my house whence I came out. And when he cometh, he findeth it swept and garnished" (Lu. 11:24-25).

No, hell is not going to be a place where you meet your friends and stand around the fire keeping warm. Hell *will not be a luminous place*. It will be a place of utter darkness. It will occupy all dead space that once comprised our present universe. Each individual will be completely alone. No stars, moons, or earthlike planets will remain here. It will be a place where the selfish soul can remain blind forever.

"But the day of the Lord will come as a thief in the night; in the which the heavens shall pass away with great noise, and the elements shall melt with fervent heat, the earth also and the works that are therein shall be burned up. Seeing then that all these things shall be dissolved, what manner of persons ought ye to be in all holy conversation and godliness" (II Peter 3:10,11)?

"And death and hell were cast into the lake of fire. This is the second death" (Rev. 20:14). God is going to leave the wicked in the dark. "And shall cast them into a furnace of fire: there shall be wailing and gnashing of teeth. Then shall the righteous shine forth as the sun in the kingdom of their Father. Who hath ears to hear, let him hear (Mt. 13:42-43).

"As therefore the tares are gathered and burned in the fire; so shall it be in the end of this world" (Mt. 13:40). Failure to understand Jesus as Lord is going to leave the sinners by themselves in this darkened underworld—alone! These spirits will forever live without the "light" of God again. Satan's spiritual kingdom is now expanded to include all darkness as the final punishment for the wicked.

God allowed Egypt to be great in order to temper his own people (Rom. 9:17), just as He created the whole universe to arrive at the perfect formula for life upon this earth (Gen. 1:26). Once man is perfected, God will be finished with the stars, the sun, the moons, and all other materialistic matter (See Rev. 21:23). Men will be given new bodies to live in this new spiritual universe, void of all material except for the most precious. This creation has produced some beautiful by-products, such as gold and other gems. God will retain these to adorn his heavenly throne.

Scripture indicates records will be kept as a remembrance of all events that happened on earth (Rev. 20:12). Scripture tells us Jesus retains the nailprints on his hands and feet (Lu. 24:40; Jn. 20:27; Zach. 12:10, 13:6).

"For as the new heavens and the new earth, which I will make, shall remain before me, saith the Lord, so shall your seed and name remain. And it shall come to pass, that from one new moon to another, and from one sabbath to another, shall all flesh come to worship before me, saith the Lord. And they shall go forth and look upon the carcasses of the men that have transgressed against me: for their worm shall not die, neither shall their fire be quenched; and they shall be abhorring unto all flesh" (Isa. 66:22-24). Should anyone rise up in the future to challenge the position of God, he will be made to review the horrors of what happened when Satan did.

Satan, and those who attuned themselves to him, are simply going to be left behind. Meanwhile, at *this* very moment, Jesus is preparing new mansions in heaven that await the redeemed (Jn. 14:3).

The lessons of this earth will be a constant reminder for those who reside with Jesus. We will be constantly aware of the terror and disruption when God was directly challenged. We have global communication right now on earth that widens our view of that epic struggle. A very long struggle with telling clues still etched in the earth's fossil record.

Few thinking men can deny that this earth has undergone disruptions and a violent past. The fossil evidence does not indicate a perfect plan. What we see in earths fossil record is a struggle that God has had with Satan and the earth has been their centerpiece.

The Bible does not talk about redemption for fallen angels, only the redemption of man. The human creature seems to have a special place with God, and that special position is based on love. What is often lost in this general term is that the epitome of love is *trust*. The way you learn to trust the Lord is entirely up to you. Do you trust the Lord through sickness, tragedies, death, and oppression. The first sin transpired because of lack of trust.

Love transformation comes into one's own soul when he learns the ways of God. That is why we came to this earth in the flesh. Here is the place we learn to love God back. Zeal for God is a wanting desire (Rom. 10:2). James tells that zeal alone is not enough (Ja 2:17). Salvation connects our soul with spiritual confirmation. This we must work out for ourselves. How each individual does this has to be directed by themselves for them to grow and become an independent thinking individual. No two people are exactly alike.

The Bible can be a study in some of God's attributes. God can be known only by His attributes, even from the things that he has made (Rom. 1:20). It does take faith to transform spiritually the physical attributes of God. He leaves a record about His physical attributes in the Bible if one is diligent enough to look for it.

Spiritual associations are very difficult until the full extent of God's workings are known. Until one finds God's spiritual foundation (love), it is very hard to focus on exactly what He is saying. When we focus on that which is spiritual we have to separate God from the devil because both dwell in the same realm on earth. While we are earthbound, the spiritual relationship vacillates from weak to strong, depending on how much faith is prevalent at any one time. Should one develop a working with the spirit, they are forever gaining insight about truth. This is crude but true; read the Bible and let God click the truth of it into your mind.

God will not work on you this way when one approaches the subject with preconceived ideas. Those spiritually endowed are: "Rejoicing in hope, patient in tribulation; continuing instant in prayer" (Rom. 12:12). The transformation from the material to the spiritual grows until one day you find yourself "blessing them which persecute you" (Rom. 12:14). One does this knowing that we grow through chastisement.

Those with the Spirit let God guide their personal lives. They realize they need some divine guidance to arrive through Satan's world. John said: "He that saith, I know him and keepeth not his commandments, is a liar, and the truth is not in him (1 Jn. 2:4).

To know you are loved by God takes one through the trials of this life without fear.

They do rejoice who know God cares enough to "chasteneth" them (Heb. 12:6). Knowing is what makes life much more abundant—and a lot more enduring to live.

EPILOGUE

There is no such a thing as a perfect agenda. The only one who ever tried to do this wound up on a cross between two thieves. It is very difficult to examine the future and get it all exactly right, but the discrepancies are from a man. God wants us to trust him and that is the reason for prophesy. He sure gives a lot to relate to. Only God lived perfect within Satan's dominion. Being so, He left us a good road map to follow: "Though he were a Son, yet learned he obedience by the things which he suffered; and being made perfect, he became the author of eternal salvation unto all them that obey him" (Heb. 5:8-9).

Jesus lived the same as we until He was perfected when he received the Holy Spirit. Afterwards the Spirit remained exclusively with Him (Jn. 1:33), until he gave it up at the cross. Today that same Spirit represents Him to those who endeavor to obey. Each of us has a soul, and it is our duty to return that soul to God with an attitude that is acceptable. The ancients developed a better mind power than we do today, but it was directed towards moving one hundred and twenty ton blocks. Perhaps because they had more time to work with brain power.

God made promises to three groups of people. The children of Israel. Ishmael, and the Gentiles. He condemned others like the descendants of Ham and Japeth. After the Jews rejected Jesus He took His message to his "other sheep" who are lost. We discussed how Bible prophecy makes it clear who those "other sheep" are.

Satan has a way of first confusing the truth until the people cry out for change. This gives him a welcome opening as uninformed men use their lofty earthly stations to put their own twist on God's holy principles.

We saw where Old Testament literature underwent change. Couple this with the fact that Satan did the same thing to the Moslem sect when he introduced the Koran. They say angel Gabriel is supposed to have given Mohammed the Koran.

Now we have the Book of Mormon giving a counterfeit message that leads people away from the very purposes of Jesus Christ. Those who embrace it receive a blur about God.

As for now, it seems almost absurd that the friendly Mormon people could do anyone any harm, but they have demonstrated in the past they can quickly alter course and become viciously evil when their lives are threatened. Why take a chance. Put yourself in position to be caught up in the clouds and out of harms way.

When the Jews added the Book of Deuteronomy and made up their Torah it did hide the works God was to do with the lost ten tribes of Israel. As we can see, there was a lot to be done through these lost people. This move by the Jews shut the rest of the world out too. We of late have not been privileged to know how the lost ten tribes fits the plan of God. We were given the clues in the Bible if we apply them properly. Jesus tell us to make that distinction between the wheat and the tares. We stop at thinking the choice is between to good and the bad, when it is more true to think about the adoption. The Bible explains the adoption back in Genesis chapter 48. No one can be saved unless they are adopted into the House of Israel. The salvation blessings were only promised to that one family (Rom. 8:15).

"Preach the word; be instant in season, out of season; reprove, rebuke, exhort with all longsuffering and doctrine" (II Tim. 4:2). God often speaks with other men through you (Mt. 10:19-20).